Serving the Country and the Communist Cause

Titles of Related Interest

ANDROPOV,Y.V.	Speeches and Writings
BREZHNEV,L.I.	A Short Biography: Workers of all Countries Unite How it was: The War and Post-war Reconstruction in the Soviet Union Selected Speeches and Writings on Foreign Affairs Virgin Lands: Two Years in Kazakhstan, 1954-5 Memoirs Socialism, Democracy and Human Rights
BORISOV,O.B.	Modern Diplomacy of Capitalist Powers
CHERNENKO,K.	Selected Speeches and Writings
GORSHKOV,S.G.	Sea Power of the State
GROMYKO,A.A.	Only for Peace: Selected Speeches and Writings
KOSYGIN,A.N.	Selected Speeches and Writings
LEBEDEV,N.I.	A New State in International Relations Great October and Today's World
PATOLICHEV,N.S.	Measures of Maturity; My Early Life
PONOMAREV,B.N.	Selected Speeches and Writings
SUSLOV,M.A.	Selected Speeches and Writings
TIKHONOV,N.A.	Selected Speeches and Writings

Serving the Country and the Communist Cause

by

D. F. USTINOV

Marshal of the Soviet Union

Translated by

PENNY DOLE

PERGAMON PRESS

OXFORD · NEW YORK · TORONTO · SYDNEY · PARIS · FRANKFURT

U.K.	Pergamon Press Ltd., Headington Hill Hall, Oxford OX3 0BW, England
U.S.A.	Pergamon Press Inc., Maxwell House, Fairview Park, Elmsford, New York 10523, U.S.A.
CANADA	Pergamon Press Canada Ltd., Suite 104, 150 Consumers Rd., Willowdale, Ontario M2J 1P9, Canada
AUSTRALIA	Pergamon Press (Aust.) Pty. Ltd., P.O. Box 544, Potts Point, N.S.W. 2011, Australia
FRANCE	Pergamon Press SARL, 24 rue des Ecoles, 75240 Paris, Cedex 05, France
FEDERAL REPUBLIC OF GERMANY	Pergamon Press GmbH, Hammerweg 6, D-6242 Kronberg-Taunus, Federal Republic of Germany

First edition 1983

British Library Cataloguing in Publication Data

Ustinov, D.F.
Serving the Country and the Communist Cause
1. Soviet Union—Military policy
I. Title
355'.0335'47 UA770

ISBN 0–08–028174–5

PUBLISHER'S NOTE TO READERS

As is well known, Pergamon Press have for some time been publishing books by senior Soviet politicians (Politbureau members) for the purpose of enabling interested English-speaking readers to know their views and opinions about international and domestic affairs.

The views expressed in this book are those of the author and not necessarily those of the Publisher.

Printed in Great Britain by A. Wheaton & Co. Ltd., Exeter

Contents

Introduction

The armed forces of the Soviet Union, like the entire Soviet people, live and work under the beneficial influence of the ideas of the XXVIth Congress of the Communist Party of the Soviet Union. In sub-units, units and ships and in all military collectives urgent and purposeful work is being carried out in fulfilment of the plans of the Congress and on steadily improving preparation for and increase in military and naval preparedness.

The XXVIth Congress of the CPSU became an important milestone in the heroic history of Lenin's party, of the Soviet people, in the history of the world socialist system, the national liberation and international communist and working-class movements. It marked a new high watermark in the progress of the Soviet Union towards communism, illuminated with the light of collective wisdom the prospects of the further, comprehensive development of our mature socialist society and outlined ways to preserve and strengthen universal peace. The Congress showed us convincingly that our Party is worthily fulfilling its leading and guiding role in society and is following, in its close unity with the people, the true Leninist course.

The programme of communist construction elaborated at the XXVIth Party Congress was given concrete form by the November (1981) Plenum of the Central Committee of the CPSU and was strengthened by the laws of the USSR passed at the sixth session of the tenth USSR Supreme Soviet on state plans for economic and social development for 1982 and the eleventh five-year plan.

Everything outlined in these plans expresses the fundamental, vital interests of the people. While implementing them persistently, the Soviet people are displaying extreme vigilance towards the aggressive machinations of imperialism. Through the fault of the warlike circles in the USA and NATO who have been steering a course towards the destruction of *détente* and the achievement of military superiority over the USSR and the Warsaw Pact countries, the international scene at the beginning of the eighties has become highly sensitive. Faced with a growing military threat from imperialism, the Soviet Union has been forced to strengthen its defence capability and to maintain the armed forces in a constant state of military preparedness.

The forces know full well what great responsibility is vested in them by the Party and the people. They are working tirelessly to improve their skill in manning powerful military technology and weaponry, improve their ground, air and sea training, their morale and political competence, and striving in exemplary fashion to solve military training problems and to strengthen organisation and discipline. A clear expression of the patriotism of the Soviet forces is to be found in their active participation in socialist competition.

The high evaluation given the armed forces at the XXVIth Party Congress by the General Secretary of the Central Committee of the CPSU, President of the Praesidium of the USSR Supreme Soviet, President of the USSR Defence Council and Marshal of the Soviet Union, Comrade Brezhnev, inspired new successes in military and political training and in the daily service of the forces. Together with the people, army, navy and air force personnel are striving to steadily increase the power and glory of their country. The Soviet forces, closely rallied as they are around the Communist Party and its Leninist Central Committee, are fulfilling their patriotic and international duty with honour. They are worthily carrying on the heroic traditions of older generations, are vigilantly protecting the peaceful labour of the people and the great socialist gains and faithfully serving their country and the cause of communism.

1

In the Name of Communism and Peace on Earth

1. The USSR—the Vanguard of Social Progress and Bulwark of International Security

From its first act of foreign policy—Lenin's Decree on Peace—to the Peace Programme for the Eighties which was adopted by the XXVIth Congress of the CPSU, the Soviet state has unswervingly adhered to the cause of peace, freedom and security for the people. "Our struggle to strengthen peace and relax international tension", Comrade Brezhnev declared in a report to the Central Committee of the CPSU at the XXVIth Congress of the Party, "is first of all a struggle to secure for the Soviet people the necessary external conditions for solving the constructive problems before us. In so doing we are also solving a problem of a truly universal character. For there is, at the moment, no more vital or more important question for any people than that of the preservation of peace, the guarantee of the primary right of every man—the right to life."[1]

The present international scene is marked by an increase in the struggle between the two tendencies in world politics. The Soviet Union, together with the other countries of the socialist community, are firmly and consistently steering a course towards restraint of the arms race, the strengthening of peace and *détente* and defence of the sovereign rights and freedoms of the peoples. In this they are opposed by the USA and their accomplices who are set to undermine *détente*, to step up the arms race and suppress the national liberation struggle.

[1] *Materials from the XXVIth Congress of the CPSU,* Moscow, 1981, pp. 4–5.

This confrontation is distinguished by extreme tension. Aggressive circles in the USA and NATO are aiming, in whatever way they can, to destroy the military strategic balance which has developed and to achieve military superiority over the USSR and the Warsaw Pact countries. They are attempting to reduce the socialist countries to a state of siege and to push back the forces of national and social liberation.

The US administration, having taken the path of political adventurism, resorts all the more frequently to a frankly warlike vocabulary. Their highly-placed representatives assert with cynical disregard for the fate of people in general that "there are more important things than peace", and that the so-called "limited" nuclear war is quite permissible and that it is possible to gain victory by it. Declarations resound all the more loudly to the effect that NATO "must be stronger than anything else in the world", that the USA and its partners must arm themselves more intensively, thus putting constant pressure on the Soviet Union and other socialist countries.

The Washington administration is trying to cast doubt on everything positive that has been jointly achieved in the sphere of Soviet–American relations during the seventies. The people invested with state authority in one of the strongest world powers—the USA, as Comrade Brezhnev observed—speak far more willingly about confrontation than *détente*, about the use of trade for purposes of military strategy than about peaceful, mutually advantageous co-operation, about dictation from a position of military superiority rather than agreement based on parity and equal security, about the making of ever newer military bases rather than stamping out seats of conflict by joint efforts, about its increasing military presence in different parts of the world rather than about curbing the arms race, about "arming up" rather than limiting or prohibiting certain kinds of weaponry and about the creation of yet newer, more destructive, means of mass annihilation.

Moreover they not only talk about this line but put it into practice. The Treaty on the Limitation of Strategic Arms signed as far back as the summer of 1979 has not yet been brought into force. The USA, and after it several other Western powers, blocked agreement at the Vienna talks on mutual armed forces and arms reductions in Central Europe. Washington, in its one-sided way, refused to discuss the restrictions of military activity in the Indian Ocean and limitation of the supply and delivery of conventional weapons. It avoided, to the best of its ability, talks on a total and universal nuclear test ban. The USA has still not ratified the treaties signed several years ago on the limitation of underground nuclear tests and underground nuclear explosions for peaceful purposes. The Treaty on the Limitation of Antiballistic Missiles Systems that came into force in 1972 is being undermined.

This shows nothing but contempt for the peaceful aspirations of all peoples, a direct opposition to *détente*. But surely there are no reasonable alternatives to *détente*. Those political leaders in the West to whom a sober approach to the objective realities of the modern world is not alien understand this well. The broad masses of the population in the capitalist countries are becoming ever more deeply aware of this. In a number of West European countries belonging to NATO, and in the USA itself, an anti-war, anti-nuclear missile movement has been unfolding—an unequivocal answer to the dangerous militaristic policies of the leaders of this bloc.

The struggle for *détente*, for improvement of the international political climate, is an extremely complex and difficult matter demanding great restraint and firmness, purposefulness and persistence. "Anyone who thought", Lenin pointed out, "that it would be easy to achieve peace, that one only has to mention peace and the bourgeoisie will bring it to us on a plate, is completely naïve."[2]

The ever deeper understanding by the mass of the people of the vital need to curb aggressive imperialistic forces and of the irreversibility of the catastrophic consequences to which nuclear war could lead if these forces managed to unleash it is arousing millions of people throughout the world to become actively involved in the solution of fundamental questions of peace policy and of course of the most important and most pressing of them—how to preserve peace.

Our country has done much to avert war. With its high-principled and constructive approach to international affairs, its readiness on a basis of equality and mutually advantageous co-operation with other countries, its consistency and firmness in conducting peace policies, the Soviet Union has gained great prestige and gratitude from the peoples of the world. All people of goodwill see it as the well-tried vanguard of mankind's social progress, the indestructible bulwark of international security and peace.

The USSR proceeds from the assumption that the preservation and strengthening of peace cannot be separated from restraint of the arms race. It has been doing and continues to do everything in its power to lessen the threat of another world war. The foreign policy programme put forward at the XXVIth Congress of the CPSU has become an important, restorative, and stabilising motive force in world politics. It contains a comprehensive set of peace proposals. That is, consolidation of confidence-building

[2] V.I. Lenin, *Poln. sobr. soch.*, vol. 35, p. 116.

measures in the military sphere and extension of the area of their application; an immediate resumption of Soviet-American talks on the limitation and reduction of strategic arms; the establishment of a moratorium on stationing new medium-range ballistic missiles in Europe for NATO countries, the USSR and others.

The Communist Party and the Soviet government are working persistently to bring about this programme. The urgent realisation of its proposals has become especially topical in view of the relentless growth of imperialist aggression and the intensification of US and NATO military preparations. The address of the USSR Supreme Soviet "to the parliaments and peoples of the world" met with an ardent response in the four corners of the earth. It emphasised that "the guarantee of peace was, is and will continue to be the chief goal of Soviet foreign policy . . .

"In our nuclear age dialogue and talks are equally necessary to all just as peace, security and confidence in the future are necessary to all."[3]

In the present situation, as never before, we need to be circumspect, to weigh up each foreign policy move, to make honest and at the same time daring efforts in the name of international security and peace. All peaceful Soviet peace initiatives answer these demands in full. They are based on the principle of parity and equal security for all parties wishing to overcome the strain in international relations, to progress towards greater *détente*, and to find concrete and practical solutions to the problems of limitation of the arms race. The USSR considers that there is no sphere of disarmament and no category of weapon on which it would be impossible to come to an agreement.

The aspiration of the Soviet Union to curb the arms race and avert a nuclear catastrophe has received new convincing confirmation at the XXXVIth Session of the UN General Assembly which passed a series of most vital resolutions following the proposals put forward by the USSR. A central place among them was occupied by the Declaration of the UN General Assembly on the prevention of nuclear catastrophe. It was passed by the overwhelming majority of delegates to the session, despite attempts by the USA and other NATO countries, who voted against the resolution, to cast doubt on the necessity for such a declaration. This resolution recorded that any state or statesman first to resort to the use of nuclear weapons would be committing the gravest crime against humanity.

Another Soviet proposal was also seconded by the overwhelming majority of votes—that was to conclude a treaty banning the placement of

[3] *Pravda*, 24 June, 1981.

any kind of weapon in space. The UN General Assembly passed for the first time in history a resolution brought by the German Democratic Republic on behalf of all the fraternal socialist countries, condemning production of the neutron bomb.

The passing by the international community of documents on disarmament, many of which were based on ideas put forward by the Soviet Union, was yet another convincing demonstration of the fact that the principled peace policy of the USSR defined at the XXVIth Congress of the CPSU and expressed in the Peace Programme for the Eighties is winning the approval and support of most of the countries of the world.

The visit to the Federal German Republic in November 1981 of the General Secretary of the Central Committee of the CPSU, President of the Praesidium of the USSR Supreme Soviet, Comrade Brezhnev, was of great political consequence in the practical accomplishment of the Soviet peace programme. The new Soviet proposals put forward during the visit offer a constructive programme for the reduction of nuclear arms in Europe. They are based on a most important principle—the principle of parity and equal security for all parties—and are regarded by the progressive international community as a new weighty contribution from the USSR to the cause of peace and security for the peoples.

Comrade Brezhnev's visit to the Federal Republic of Germany was of special significance for East–West relations at that difficult stage of world development. One of the chief conclusions that follows from the Soviet–West German talks is that states, irrespective of their social system or membership in any particular military alliances, should make every effort to continue working together for the consolidation of peace and restoration of the climate of *détente* and trust. And it is important that this should be a guideline for the practical policy of all states.

The Soviet Union intends to achieve positive results at the Soviet–American talks in Geneva on the limitation of nuclear weapons in Europe. It is speaking out for an early resumption of talks between the USSR and USA on the limitation of strategic arms in an effort to preserve everything positive that has already been achieved in this sphere. The USSR considers that the proposals introduced from 1978 to 1981 by the socialist countries—participants in the talks—will serve to overcome the *impasse* at the Vienna talks on the mutual reduction of armed forces and arms in Central Europe.

In its consistent and steadfast struggle to curb the arms race and negotiate for disarmament, peace and security for all peoples, the Soviet Union acts in full accord with the other socialist countries. "The greatest good for all mankind is that the united might of the socialist countries and their active policy in defence of peace are cooling the aggressive ambitions of the imperialists, and are creating a decisive barrier to the unleashing of a nuclear world war by aggressors", said Comrade Brezhnev. "This result from the policy of the socialist countries is benefiting the whole of mankind."[4]

Equitable, equal, truly brotherly relations bind the USSR with the states of the socialist community—Bulgaria, Hungary, Vietnam, the German Democratic Republic, Cuba, Laos, Mongolia, Poland, Rumania and Czechoslovakia. The socialist community has become the most powerful community of peoples that history has ever known. No other community can compare with it either in rates of economic growth or the scale and importance of the social tasks being decided or in its influence on world development.

The CPSU and the Soviet government are working tirelessly to strengthen unity and extend and improve co-operation between the fraternal countries in all spheres. They are doing what they can to consolidate the international position of the socialist community and to increase their combined efforts in the struggle for peace and social progress. The General Secretary of the Central Committee of the CPSU, President of the Praesidium of the USSR Supreme Soviet, Comrade Brezhnev, made a major contribution to this work and to the creative development of revolutionary theory and practice for constructing a new society.

The co-operation of the socialist countries is founded on loyalty to Marxism–Leninism, to socialist internationalism and to their common fundamental interests and aims. Internationalism is one of the chief sources of socialist strength. It is an important condition for the successful development of each of the fraternal countries, for the confident advance of our whole community. This is the dialectics of the development and defence of the new community.

The mutual relations of the fraternal peoples and states are imbued with sincerity, the deepest trust and a spirit of real equality, friendship and comradeship. The Constitution of the USSR proclaims relations of friendship, co-operation and mutual aid with the socialist countries as the cornerstone of Soviet foreign policy. And in their constitutions the majority of fraternal states emphasise ideas of friendship and co-operation with the Soviet Union. The communist and workers' parties constitute the guiding and organising strength of the socialist community. Their constant interaction

[4] L.I. Brezhnev, *Leninskim kursom: Rechi i stat'i*, Moscow, 1973, vol. 2, p. 588.

results in a principled unity of views on all the major problems of socioeconomic development, international policy and co-ordinated friendly efforts to resolve the tasks involved in the construction of socialism and communism.

Latterly the fraternal countries have had to conduct this construction in worsening international conditions. The world economic situation has deteriorated. The process of *détente* has been hampered by the efforts of imperialist reaction and its stooges. The USA and NATO are whipping up the arms race. The ideological struggle in the world arena is intensifying. Attempts are being made by reactionary powers to break the international solidarity of the socialist states, to shatter the foundation of socialism from within.

They made a special bid during events in the Polish People's Republic to destroy the socialist system in that country, to restore the bourgeois order and to tear her away from the socialist community, thus attempting to revise the results of the Second World War and postwar development.

By drawing support from the working class and all the patriotic forces of Poland, the constitutional Polish authorities organised and led the attack against the counter-revolution. As a result the situation in the country is stabilising. In so acting, the Polish communists and all the true patriots of Poland have obtained the full support of the fraternal peoples and states.

The bonds that unite the countries of the socialist community are indissoluble and life-giving. The strengthening of these bonds, the close co-ordination in the construction of the new society and in its defence fully answer both the national and international interests of the fraternal peoples.

At the present time when the reactionary forces of imperialism and their accomplices have begun a massive offensive on *détente*, on peace and the rights of peoples, the joint action of the socialist countries in defence of their very great values and in solving creative tasks is more important than ever before. Such unity is a guarantee of success in the fight against imperialism and reaction, a guarantee of the fuller use of the advantages of the socialist economic system and of opportunities revealed by scientific progress.

The even greater political co-operation and development of the entire system of bilateral and multilateral relationships between the fraternal parties and states including the Warsaw Treaty Organisation are steadily serving to reinforce the unity of the socialist nations. Its Political Consultative Committee first and foremost plays a huge rôle in the activity of this purely defensive organisation in European and, on the whole, in international affairs, in the struggle for peace, the preservation and strengthening of *détente* and the reduction in levels of military confrontation in Europe and other areas of the planet. Initiatives put forward at sessions of the Political Consultative Committee in Bucharest, Moscow and Warsaw have made a major contribution to strengthening peace and international security.

The political co-operation of the socialist countries is a living, creative process. It is constantly being enriched, acquiring new fruitful forms. Regular contacts between leaders of the fraternal parties and states occupy a most important place in it. The friendly meetings and discussions that take place in the Crimea are playing a special rôle in the practical implementation of these contacts. The most important tasks in developing co-operation between the socialist states are discussed during these meetings and further steps agreed on for consolidating peace and international security.

A large contribution to increasing political co-operation between the fraternal parties and states is made by the regular exchange of party–government delegations, conferences of Secretaries of Central Committees on international questions and on matters of ideological and party organisational work which broaden the links between party organisations at all levels—from the republics, territories and provinces to regions and vast enterprises. Associations between government bodies, public organisations and industrial collectives are also successfully developed.

The economic co-operation of the socialist states serves to help construct the new society, to guarantee the security of the fraternal countries and to preserve and strengthen peace. By opening up a wide vista onto the advantages of the socialist method of production within the framework of the socialist community, it ensures the dynamic and stable development of the fraternal countries. The more than thirty-year activity of the Council for Mutual Economic Assistance (Comecon or CMEA) is significant in this respect. The industrial production of the Council's member states from 1975 to 1980 has grown more than three times as fast as the average world level. And the national income which has increased by two-thirds over the last decade is almost twice that of the developed capitalist countries.

A steady rise in production, the acceleration of scientific progress and a constant increase in the well-being of the people based on this are ensured by socialist economic integration. It embraces ever newer spheres, attains ever higher rates and is embodied in the fulfilment of long-term target-oriented programmes. The building of certain very important projects is evidence of successes in joint work. Such projects as the "Soyuz" gas pipeline, the "Mir" power supply system, the Ust'-Ilimsk cellulose plant, the "Erdenet" dressing complex in Mongolia, the nickel mills in Cuba and many others. The programme "Interspace" is a clear symbol of the fruitful friendship and co-operation between the fraternal peoples and states. Everything that has been done by the socialist countries in economic development and in raising the standard of living represents, as Comrade Brezhnev emphasised, a whole era.

Consequently the new proposals for further developing the economic co-operation of the socialist states are being put into action. These proposals received ardent support in the fraternal countries. It is a question of converting the forthcoming two five-year plans into a period of intensive industrial and technological co-operation between the socialist states and of supplementing the co-ordination of plans with agreement on the economic policy as a whole. The most topical questions of economic co-operation are integration of economic mechanisms, the development of direct links between the ministries, associations and enterprises participating in this co-operation and the creation of joint firms, etc. The solution of these questions is called for in order to promote the comprehensive expansion of economic co-operation between the socialist countries, the raising of efficiency and the further pooling of our efforts and resources.

Greater co-operation in the economic, scientific and technical spheres helps satisfy the needs of all the fraternal states and the growth of the economic power and defence capability of the socialist community and increases the possibilities of real socialism by curbing the international forces of reaction and aggression.

The most important component in the combined struggle of the socialist countries for peace and social progress is the coordination of their efforts in the sphere of ideological work. Our common inheritance in the communist world-outlook and our loyalty to Marxism–Leninism—the all-conquering doctrine, under whose banner all modern revolutionary forces are rallying—make this work very effective.

In such circumstances the attacking character and the purposefulness of all ideological work and of all political, educational work with people and the effective co-operation of the mass media in the socialist countries are of particular importance. The truth about real socialism, about its profound humanism, and its unwavering dedication to peace and at the same time its persuasive exposure of the incurable vices and ills of capitalism and of the reactionary, aggressive nature of imperialism, are a mighty weapon in the struggle against our class enemies.

Of great import in guaranteeing the security of each and every fraternal country and the entire socialist confraternity is co-operation in the sphere of defence. "We are giving this matter our undivided attention," Comrade Brezhnev said, "this primarily concerns relations with the participants of the Warsaw Pact which is a powerful instrument for co-operation in policy and defence between the socialist countries."[5]

From year to year the many-sided co-operation of the Soviet Union with the countries of socialist co-operation flourishes and strengthens. A combined search to find a better combination of national and community interests and an effective solution to the great tasks of constructing socialism and communism is being tirelessly carried out.

The friendship of the fraternal countries, imbued as it is with the spirit of socialist internationalism, is becoming ever deeper and more productive. The socialist world has made such relations between states a reality; these are in fact relations between peoples, relations in which millions and millions of people directly participate. This is the general gain of socialism, its great service to mankind.

The USSR is constantly developing its relations with those socialist countries who are not members of the Warsaw Pact or of the Council for Mutual Economic Assistance. The friendship of the Soviet Union with the Socialist Federative Republic of Yugoslavia has deep roots. Soviet–Yugoslav co-operation is advancing in many directions. The USSR expresses its firm solidarity with the struggle of the Korean People's Democratic Republic for the peaceful democratic unification of their country without foreign interference. Our country is anxious to strengthen and enrich its ties with the Republic.

Loyalty to socialist internationalism and mutually advantageous co-operation and aid based on equality give a powerful impetus to the development of the socialist countries and lead not only to the forming but to the multiplying of their strength in the struggle to build a new society, for peace and social progress. This result is confirmed by the very rich revolutionary practice of the modern world. Objective reality shows us visibly what departure from the unshakeable foundations of Marxism–Leninism and distortion of the principles of socialism and its essence in domestic and foreign policy can lead to. The experience of the Chinese People's Republic in its socioeconomic development over the last two decades may serve as a bitter lesson of this kind.

Our Party's just criticisms of Maoism—its petit-bourgeois and nationalistic character—were fully confirmed by time. The present Chinese leaders, as was shown by the VIth Plenum of the Central Com-

[5] L.I. Brezhnev, *Leninskim kursom,* vol. 2, p. 124.

mittee of the Chinese Communist Party held in June 1981, regard Maoism, as before, as the basis of their ideology and politics. A number of anti-Soviet objectives have been reaffirmed in the PRC's policy in the international arena. This policy is directed at struggle with the USSR, at aggravation of the international situation and ever closer collaboration with the most aggressive imperialistic circles.

As far as the Soviet Union is concerned, it is in favour of normalising relations with the Chinese People's Republic and is steadily pursuing a policy of peace and good-neighbourliness. This policy answers both the interests of the whole world and the real interests of the Chinese people for whom the Soviet people unfailingly feel respect and friendship.

The USSR and other countries of the socialist community are perpetually concerned with the consolidation of all anti-imperialistic, progressive forces in the struggle for peace and social progress. They give primary attention to the development of mutually advantageous economic and technological co-operation between countries who have freed themselves from the colonial yoke and first of all with states who are socialistically oriented, countries that have chosen the path of socialist development. These countries have reliable and loyal friends in the states of the socialist community, natural allies in the struggle against imperialism and for national independence, peace and social progress.

Soviet co-operation with the newly-independent countries embraces many different spheres—politics and the economy, inter-party links and defence, culture and tourism and the training of national personnel. Over the last few years the Soviet Union has concluded treaties of friendship and co-operation with Angola, Ethiopia, Mozambique, Afghanistan, the People's Democratic Republic of Yemen, Syria and the People's Republic of the Congo. One of the first treaties was signed with India in 1971. The USSR has trading relations with more than eighty states in Asia, Africa and Latin America. Commodity turnover in trade with them has more than tripled over the last decade and continues to grow.

In an attempt to hold back development of the revolutionary process at any price and to isolate the liberated countries from the Soviet Union and all socialist co-operation, imperialism is resorting to crude forms of pressure, blackmail and direct political subversion. Cynically trampling on the rights and expectations of the peoples, it aspires to represent their struggle for emancipation as a manifestation of "international terrorism", and the help given the liberation movements by the socialist countries is depicted as a form of participation in them. Under this false assumption the Washington administration is hoping, by way of encouraging internal counter-revolution in the liberated countries and aggression from without, to make short work of the national liberation movements.

This method is not new. And the goal it serves is perfectly obvious. That is, to retrieve the international positions lost by imperialism, to give it back its rôle of master of peoples' destinies and to erect a barrier to progressive reform in the world. And imperialism sees the socialist community and its aid to the liberated countries as the chief obstacle to the achievement of this aim. Hence attempts to distort and to slander this aid.

Respecting, as they do, the inalienable rights of peoples to self-determination, the Soviet Union and the other socialist states do not interfere in the domestic affairs of the liberated countries, nor do they seek any advantage for themselves. The aid and support of the socialist community helps promote progressive socioeconomic and cultural reforms in the liberated countries and helps preserve their sovereignty and strengthen their independence in the face of the half-formed neocolonialist intentions of imperialism. Aid is used to strengthen defence capability and the USSR, together with the other fraternal countries, renders such aid to the liberated countries on request.

The Soviet Union has always been opposed to the export of revolution. But we cannot agree and never will agree to the export of counter-revolution. This is our position of principle. Our attitude to the events in Afghanistan is based on it. Imperialism has been attempting to bring about the export of counter-revolution to that country. Such a situation has forced the government of Afghanistan to turn to the USSR for help. And this help was given them. The General Secretary of the Central Committee of the People's Democratic Party of Afghanistan, Babrak Karmal, observed that "had it not been for the help given to heroic Afghanistan by the mighty Soviet Union, there would be no revolutionary, free, independent and non-aligned Afghanistan today."[6]

This declaration clearly shows how false the attempts of imperialistic propaganda are in representing the temporary deployment into Afghanistan of a Soviet limited military contingent as some kind of "intervention". This step is in full accordance with the UN Charter. The vital need to do this and its timeliness were once more confirmed by the US President's cynical declaration in 1981 to the effect that bands invading Afghan territory from outside were being armed by the USA

[6] *Speeches of welcome at the XXVIth Congress of the CPSU from communist, workers', national-democrat and socialist parties,* Moscow, 1981, p. 307.

and that military help from Washington to these bands would continue to grow.

As regards the withdrawal of the limited contingent of Soviet forces from the Democratic Republic of Afghanistan, this problem can be resolved on the basis of a political settlement of the situation around Afghanistan in accordance with the programme set out by the government of the Democratic Republic of Afghanistan on 14 May 1980 and 24 August 1981. The USSR is ready to withdraw its forces by agreement with the Afghan government. For this to happen the despatch of counter-revolutionary bands into Afghanistan must be completely stopped and the necessary reliable guarantees drawn up against any further intervention. The Soviet Union has already demonstrated that it sticks to its word when in June 1980 it withdrew, by agreement with the Afghan government, those Soviet military units whose stay had ceased to be essential there. This became possible owing primarily to the heavy defeats suffered by the counter-revolutionary bands sent into the country.

Thanks to the internationalist aid of the Soviet Union to the Democratic Republic of Afghanistan the plans of the imperialistic and other reactionary circles to liquidate the gains of the April revolution in this country failed. The policies of the People's Democratic Party and the government of the Democratic Republic of Afghanistan are meeting the national interests of Afghanistan, strengthening the people's power and are conducive to the subsequent stabilisation of the situation in the Republic.

Comrade Brezhnev, in an answering speech when receiving the highest award of the Democratic Republic of Afghanistan—the order of "The Sun of Freedom"—again emphasised the stability of the USSR's internationalist position. ". . . just as the Soviet Union rendered help to the Afghan people in defence of their revolutionary gains," he said, "so our country is ready henceforward to help ensure a just political settlement for Afghanistan in the interests of international peace and stability."[7]

The Soviet Union regards the aspiration of young states to defend their newly acquired freedom and independence and to protect their territorial integrity from the encroachments of imperialism as lawful and just in the highest degree. This aspiration is embodied, in particular, in the activities of the Afro-Asian Solidarity Organisation for the Solidarity of Asian and African Peoples. They play an important part in uniting the efforts of the peoples of both continents in the struggle against neocolonialism, hegemonism and racism and for the preservation and consolidation of

[7] *Pravda*, 17 December, 1981.

peace. The anti-imperialistic activity of both political and economic organisations and associations of liberated countries is growing.

The non-aligned movement was and still is an important factor in international relations. Arising more than two decades ago, it now unites around one hundrd states from different continents with a population of more than 1½ milliards.

The USSR and the non-aligned states share common or close positions on many of today's fundamental problems. It is a major line of Soviet policy to develop friendship and all-round co-operation with these states. This sort of co-operation objectively serves the cause of peace and social progress.

The world communist and working-class movement is a powerful force in the anti-imperialist front. It has grown even more over the last few years. Its influence has extended. The political vanguard of the international working class—the communist and workers' parties—have gained strength. They are now active in 94 countries. Communist ideas are taking over the hearts and minds of tens and hundreds of thousands of people throughout the world.

As one of the fighting detachments of the world communist movement, the CPSU is persistently battling for the unity and cohesion of the fraternal parties, is working purposefully on further extending and deepening the all-round co-operation with them on the basis of Marxist–Leninist and proletarian internationalism. Continuous contact and the mutual exchange of information help communists from all countries in their daily work. The common struggle of the fraternal parties against aggressive imperialist policies and for socialism and peace promotes the cohesion of the world communist movement and the growth of its prestige.

The amelioration of the international political climate is a two-way process, presupposing combined efforts, the good-will of states with differing social systems and their reciprocal trust. It goes without saying that this trust cannot exist without mutuality and equal rights just as real international security cannot exist without equal security on all sides. It can only be guaranteed if, as Comrade Brezhnev observed, "all sides regard the building of lasting peace as a common task."[8]

This is an objective reality. With this in mind the CPSU forms and carries out its policy as regards the capitalist states. The most important thing about this poicy is the organic combining of the principles of peaceful coexistence, of mutually advantageous co-operation and firm rebuff to the aggressive intrigues of imperialism.

[8] *Pravda*, 3 November, 1981.

The last few years have been marked by much greater activity in the Western countries, and especially the USA, on the part of the opponents of peaceful coexistence and of improved relations with the Soviet Union and the other socialist countries. This is caused by further exacerbation of the general crisis of capitalism, the deepening of the antagonistic contradictions of bourgeois society and an increase in the struggle between imperialists for markets, raw materials and energy. Military-industrial complexes are having a stronger impact on all spheres of life in the imperialist countries and on their foreign policy. These are some of the reasons for the current aggravation of the international situation, and hence the growing threat to peace and social progress. The reactionary imperialist circles, especially those of the USA, are not making a bid to develop co-operation and mutual understanding with the Soviet Union but for the so-called "position of strength" proclaimed by Washington.

History shows that such claims in relation to the Soviet Union are always foiled. We can stand up for ourselves. And today more than ever before we have at our disposal all the essentials for this. That is why the only possible real platform for relations between socialist and capitalist countries consists in talks based on parity and equal security, peaceful coexistence and mutually advantageous co-operation.

Our country has always spoken out, and continues to speak out, in favour of developing good relations with the Western countries—equal relations based on mutual respect and trust and with consideration of mutual interests. The CPSU and the Soviet state have realistically assessed the fact that the present-day situation depends greatly on the state of Soviet–American relations and are sincerely striving to normalise relations with the USA. This sort of approach meets the interests of the peoples of both countries and of the entire world. The USSR unfailingly adheres to this belief.

During the years of *détente* much important experience has been gained from the co-operation of states with differing social systems, the USSR and USA included. The Soviet Union sees it as genuine political wisdom and as a responsibility to both the Soviet peoples and the whole of humanity to make use of this experience, to conduct matters honourably and constructively by striving to achieve the just solution of international problems through talks.

The USSR is consequently asking that the positive process begun in 1975 at the Helsinki Conference on Security and Co-operation in Europe be continued and intensified without interruption and that the principles and positions of the Final Act passed at this Conference be strictly observed. The USSR and the entire socialist community regard the Madrid follow-up conference of states—participants of the All-European Conference—in this light. If agreement were reached on convening a European conference a fundamental need would be met by strengthening trust, security and disarmament moves in Europe.

Despite the efforts of the enemies of *détente*, peaceful co-operation is still continuing between countries with differing social régimes on the European continent. This relates to both political contacts and economic, technological and cultural ties.

The course which the Soviet Union is pursuing in the international arena is a firm and consistent one aimed at developing co-operation and preserving and strengthening peace. Our devotion to the cause of peace is unshakeable. It flows from the nature of socialism. Peace is dear to the Soviet people. We need it to solve creative tasks. In tirelessly strengthening the economic and defensive might of the socialist motherland and its international prestige, the Soviet people are maintaining strict political vigilance and a readiness to defend the great gains of socialism, together with the cause of peace and social progress. Under the leadership of Lenin's party, they are confidently advancing along the road of the October Revolution.

2. An Important Stage on the Path to Communism

Socialism is having an important influence on world development with its successes in the economic sphere. In the sphere of economics and economic policy, in particular, a decisive battle is being waged in the competition of socialism with capitalism. Here, in particular, as was emphasised at the XXVIth Congress of the CPSU, the foundation is being laid for the solution of social tasks, the strengthening of our country's defence capability and the basis of an active foreign policy. It is here that essential prerequisites are created for the successful advance of Soviet society towards communism.

The Soviet economy has now reached a high level of development. The productive forces of our society are more powerful than ever before. The technological revolution is developing successfully at an increasing pace, changing the face of many sectors of production and entire branches of industry. Soviet science occupies a leading position in the most important areas of knowledge. The economic might of the country guarantees dynamic advance in all directions of the material and technical basis of communism and ensures the all-round progress of society.

A more complete and effective use of the possibilities and advantages offered by the socialist economy is attained thanks to the consistent implementation of Leninist economic policy by the CPSU. The leadership of the Party sees the national economy as at the core of its entire many-sided activity. The meaning and content of this activity are determined by the invariable demands of the CPSU programme—all in the name of mankind, for the good of mankind. This is the Party's general line. The resolutions of the XXVIth Congress of the CPSU were the creative result of this.

The November (1981) Plenum of the Central Committee of the CPSU concentrated the attention of the Party and the people on the most topical questions of economic development. Comrade Brezhnev, in his concise speech at the Plenum, comprehensively showed the great political, organisational and economic work carried out after the XXVIth Party Congress and noted the growing working and political activity of the masses. He went comprehensively into ways of further fulfilling the resolutions of the Congress and gave a detailed description and political and social evaluation of the plan for the second year and for the entire eleventh five-year plan in general.

Among some of the most important characteristics of the five-year plan are reinforcement of the social orientation of national economic development, increase in the rôle of factors of intensity and the efficiency of social production in forming stable rates of growth in the economy and the improvement of its structure and an increase in the end results of national economic activity which would outstrip the expenditure on their attainment.

Many great and complex tasks lie before the Party and the people. When talking about this, Comrade Brezhnev expressed the certainty that they would be carried out. "We have everything we need for successful work: highly-developed productive forces, the socio-political and moral unity of the Soviet people, a clear-cut strategy of advance as embodied in the resolutions of the Congress," Comrade Brezhnev observed, "so that the entire Party should be able to raise even higher the level of organisational work in the sphere of economic development."[9]

Under Party leadership the Soviet people are working enthusiastically in all fields of communist construction. Our national wealth is steadily increasing. The welfare of the people is being raised. The industrial and

[9] L.I. Brezhnev, Speech at the 16 November 1981 Plenum of the Central Committee of the CPSU: Resolution of the Plenum of the Central Committee of the CPSU, Moscow, 1981, p. 12.

technological potential of the country is growing. The sociopolitical and ideological unity of the people, the alliance of the working class, the peasantry and the intelligentsia and the friendship of all the nations and nationalities of the USSR is being consolidated. Socialist democracy is becoming more profound. The military capability of the state is becoming stronger. In all areas of construction of the materio-technical basis of communism, the USSR is moving ahead with confidence.

In accordance with its economic strategy, the Party is concentrating the efforts of the Soviet people on making the transition to *intensification,* increasing production efficiency and improving work quality by maximum use of the advantages of the socialist economic system, of the achievements of technological progress and our vast economic possibilities and reserves and by striving to economise as far as possible on all types of resources.

Fulfilment of these requirements forms the basis for solution of the main task of the current five-year plan—the securing of a further increase in the welfare of the Soviet people. It is instrumental in creating more favourable conditions for the all-round development of the individual, for highly productive work, the improvement of health and rest facilities for the Soviet people, and the development of education, science and culture—in a word, of everything that makes up our socialist way of life.

It is only possible to realise this huge and many-sided programme for raising people's welfare if it is based on the dynamic and stable development of material production. As is well known, increase in national income is the generalising indicator of such development. It will grow by 18 per cent in the eleventh five-year plan and by 1990, in accordance with the calculations, by a minimum of 1.4 times as much.

The guarantee of higher national economic results with lower expenditure of resources is completely subject to the attainment of the goals set out in the economic strategy and the successful solution to the intensification of social production, as also the acceleration of technological progress, improvement of the economic structure, the distribution of productive forces, improvements in planning and management and higher standards in management.

The Party organically links the new emphasis in the economy to higher efficiency and quality with the work being done to improve all branches of industry by speeding up technological progress and the widespread use of its achievements. It is a question of the technical re-equipment of industry, the creation and universal introduction of basically new techniques and materials and the use of high-performance energy and material-saving technology.

In the current five-year plan the renewal rate for technical equipment is roughly 1.5 times as fast. New progressive technological processes are being actively introduced and the power-to-man ratio is increasing. The quality of production is improving. More than 85,000 industrial articles are now being issued with the state seal of quality. This is three times as many as at the beginning of the tenth five-year plan.

Science is becoming increasingly effective and its association with industry more intensive. Along with the working out of theoretical problems it is concentrating its efforts in ever greater measure on solving key national economic problems and on discoveries capable of introducing really revolutionary changes into industry. Discoveries carry great possibilities in the sphere of nuclear energy, space and laser technology, electronics and chemistry and in other fields of science and technology. And it is very important that the periods for the practical assimilation of the results of scientific discoveries be reduced and that the path of inventions and innovative solutions at factories, on fields and farms should not be encumbered by sluggish attitudes, routine procedures, bureaucratic procrastination and piles of paperwork.

Realisation of the aims of technological progress produces a huge social as well as economic effect. It helps to eliminate the important differences between mental and physical work, to increase the rôle of creative functions in industrial activity, to improve working conditions and to preserve the environment.

Increased work productivity is of key importance in the intensification of the economy and in steadily raising its efficiency. This is the chief factor contributing to economic growth. Work productivity throughout the national economy must be raised in such a way, Comrade Brezhnev observed, "that it might be higher, rather than lower, than in the most developed capitalist countries. The socialist system gives us all sorts of opportunities for doing this. It is just a question of knowing how to use them correctly and of learning how to manage rationally and economically."[10]

With regard to increasing productivity in the eleventh five-year plan, a 90 per cent increase in national income has been planned. The successful solution of this task presupposes the speeding up of complex industrial mechanisation and automatisation, the introduction of the brigade form of work organisation, a consequent reduction in the proportion of low-

[10] *Pravda*, 20 December, 1981.

skilled, manual and especially heavy, physical work. An increased production output in active enterprises with a stable and even reduced work force is playing an important part. Increased productivity is unthinkable without a high degree of organisation, discipline, and responsibility in every unit, every team and on every job.

Intensification of the economy makes great demands on the entire national economy and all its branches. The Party is paying special attention to the stable, balanced growth of heavy industry. Ever newer large concerns are starting to operate in this way. During the last five-year plan the following enterprises came into production: the Sayan–Shushenskoye hydroelectric station, the Chernobyl, Kursk and Armenian atomic power stations, the Zaporozho and Uglegorsk power stations, the "Atommash" factory, the Lisichansk and Pavlodar oil refineries, the meat packing plant in Lipetsk and Zhitomir, the main Kakhovka arterial canal and many other projects. In the first year of the eleventh five-year plan the family of industrial giants was augmented by KamAZ. The planned capacity at the Leningrad atomic power station was reached ahead of schedule and new power units were introduced at a number of other large power stations. The total length of the railway systems on the "construction project of the century"—the Baikal–Amur main line—exceeded the 2200-kilometre mark in 1981.

The territorial industrial complexes in the European part of the RSFSR and in the Urals, Siberia, the Far East, Kazakhstan and Tadjikistan are developing apace. The establishment and development of a whole complex of branches as well as service industries are a characteristic feature of the present stage in their formation.

A more tangible idea of the level attained by Soviet industry today may be shown by the following facts. Soviet industry produces *per capita* more than three times as much as the world average. The general volume of Soviet industrial production constitutes one-fifth of world production. This is roughly as much as all the Western European countries put together. And the total population of these countries is one-third larger than that of the Soviet Union. The USSR leads the world in the production of oil and steel, cement and mineral fertilizers, diesel and electric locomotives and many other important items.

In concentrating the efforts of the Soviet people on solving the most current national economic problems, on eliminating existing bottlenecks and disproportions in the economy, the Party is giving primary attention to the fuel and energy complex. The job of improving its structure is very much on the agenda. It is a matter of using less oil as fuel, of replacing it with gas or coal, of speeding up development of atomic energy and continuing the search for basically new energy sources. The eleventh five-year plan represents the first stage in carrying out the Soviet energy programme worked out on Comrade Brezhnev's initiative. What links this programme up is the unified power grid of the USSR which today already covers a territory with a population of more than 220 million, and a single gas supply system. They are steadily being developed and perfected.

In metallurgy basic improvements in the quality of metal and metalware are being effected concurrent with growth in production, as are the increased output of effective types of metal production, the reduction of loss and waste and the lowering of expenditure on metal per unit of the end product. The manufacture of substitutes is being expanded. By using them instead of more traditional materials a considerable effect is produced on the economy. Thus, the use of one million tons of polymer piping can replace 5 million tons of steel piping. In this case the saving on capital investment will total 1.7 milliard roubles with approximately 0.7 milliard roubles on pipelaying work.

The transition of the national economy to intensified performance is directly dependent on the development of mechanical engineering, for machinery construction ensures the renewal of basic stocks and the technical re-equipment of different areas of the national economy. It opens the doors to all that is new and advanced, that scientific engineering thought can create. And the faster this new thinking can be assimilated into production and embodied in high-efficiency, reliable machines, instruments and technological lines, the more successful will be the solutions for raising the efficiency of the economy.

The securing of high rates of development for basic branches of industry leads to the increased output of the sorts of products that determine technical progress. This at the same time creates a solid base for increasing the manufacture of industrial consumer goods.

The Party considers it of primary importance to improve the supply of such goods to the population. Much has already been done in this direction in the first year of the eleventh five-year plan. In the current five-year plan, as a whole, the manufacture of such goods will grow by 180 milliard roubles as compared with the preceding five-year plan. This is more than the whole volume of their output in 1980. The range is being expanded and renewed, the quality of consumer goods improved and the sale of new, fashionable and reasonably priced durable goods increased. The work of commercial, public catering and consumer service establishments and all areas of service is being developed and improved.

Work, vast in scale, is being carried on in the country to ensure the interrelated, balanced development of branches forming a *single agro-industrial complex*. Almost one-third of all capital investment in the national economy is going on this. Moreover, a large part of these resources is earmarked directly for raising agricultural production, for converting agriculture into a highly developed sector of the socialist economy. The successful outcome of this task depends a great deal on how sensibly these resources are utilised. Every hectare of land, every rouble of investment and every ton of fertiliser must give the maximum return.

The Party's present agrarian policy, the foundations of which were laid by the resolutions of the March (1965) Plenum of the Central Committee of the CPSU, is the continuation and creative development of Lenin's teaching on the agrarian question in new historical conditions—those of a mature socialist society. Its subsequent realisation ensures the all-round, dynamic development and steady growth in efficiency of all branches of agriculture and is conducive to satisfying ever more fully the need of the population for high-quality food products, and of industry for raw materials.

The continuous strengthening of agricultural production potential, the further development of such specialised branches as agricultural construction, land improvement and water management, machinery construction for livestock-raising and feed production, and the microbiological industry all contribute to realising the tasks before agriculture. The economic and technological links of the village with industry are expanding. The scientific potential of agriculture is steadily growing. Work is continuing on converting the non-black-earth zone of the RSFSR into a region of highly productive arable and livestock farming.

The attainment by our agriculture of the levels projected by the XXVIth Congress of the CPSU will help to improve the food supply to the population. "The food problem, both on the economic and political plane," Comrade Brezhnev emphasised at the November (1981) Plenum of the Central Committee of the CPSU, "will be the central problem of the whole five-year plan. Its basic solution lies in a high rate of agricultural production."[11]

The complex food programme is setting out to pool all efforts in agriculture itself, in its service branches of industry and to subordinate the work

[11] L.I. Brezhnev, Speech at the 16 November 1981 Plenum of the Central Committee of the CPSU: Resolution of the Plenum of the Central Committee of the CPSU, p. 4.

of all these branches to a common ultimate goal—i.e. to guarantee the supply of food to the country. It is being worked out according to the resolution of the XXVIth Congress of the CPSU and will be included in the eleventh five-year plan. The fuller utilisation of local food reserves and of subsidiary farming facilities have been called on to play an important part in securing foodstuffs for the population.

The growth of the economic potential of the country is largely determined by the state of capital construction. Its increased effectiveness presupposes a concentration of effort on the major directives and on the initial objectives of the national economy, in the first place on those capable of ensuring the greatest growth in production. To plan and construct quickly and at the same time with high standards of quality and economy at the modern level of technology—this is what the present stage in the development of society needs. Our general rate of advance will be very dependent on fulfilment of this need and on how things go in construction.

The development and improvement of branches of the production infrastructure are of no small importance in the intensification of the economy. The Party has set itself the task of improving transport, particularly the railway. The organisation of haulage is being urgently improved, measures are being taken to ensure the rational use of rolling stock, and the reduction of demurrages of wagons, machinery and vessels. The instillation of the experience gained at the Leningrad transportation centre and by the railwaymen of the Moscow and L'vov provinces has had a significant effect in this respect.

Execution of the tasks put forward by the XXVIth Congress of the CPSU in the construction of new railway lines, the updating of technical equipment for operating railways and the ensuring of the precise coordination of all links in the transportation system is going apace. Further improvements in the transportation system and its links with other branches of the national economy will come about through the long-term comprehensive programme being worked out in accordance with the Basic Guidelines for the Economic and Social Development of the USSR for 1981–1985 and for the period up to 1990.

The attainment of good national economic results depends to a large extent on how well the economy, planning and administration are managed. While speaking about the problems involved in improving management of the economy, Comrade Brezhnev emphasised that they must be solved "taking account of the experience and creative initiative of our people, taking account of the best experience there is in the fraternal countries of socialism and also in the developed capitalist countries."[12]

Management of the economy is not just an economic matter but also a political and party one. To make it work we need to mobilise the creative potential of the whole of our society and to reveal as far as possible, and make use of, existing opportunities. Over the last few years a broad complex measure has been adopted for improving the economic mechanism. The system of planning and management is aiming all the more to increase the efficiency and quality of work and to achieve good end results for the national economy. Extensive work is being conducted on the introduction of new forms and methods of planning, new ways to evaluate the activities of working collectives and to improve the efficacy of economic levers and incentives.

The most important condition for putting into practice Party directives for increasing the efficiency of social production and work quality as a pivotal task for the national economy is to be found in the steady growth of the public activity of the masses, their interested and active participation in state and public matters. The creation and universal introduction of such a functioning system of incentives, both moral and material, that would work without a hitch and motivate people to work to peak efficiency and continuously raise the quality of production acquires more importance in this case. The civic awareness of all the Soviet people, their attitude to work and socialist ownership and their discipline and culture in work and public and everyday life must be lifted to a new level. In the final analysis, the life of every Soviet citizen today, of our entire society and of our tomorrows depend on this.

With the growth in the scale and complexity of production any show of poor management, lack of conscientiousness, carelessness or infringement of the established plans and tasks would cause a good deal of harm. It is enough to remember how great the cost of working time is today. Every minute the country produces more than 2.4 million kilowatt-hours of electric power, almost 300 tons of steel, 1.4 thousand tons of coal, approximately 800,000 cubic metres of gas and a huge quantity of other products. To waste only one minute to no purpose means to lose irretrievably the results of a total day's labour of about 200,000 workers.

A fuller and more effective use of basic production resources, the raising of return on capital investment, the economic expenditure of raw material, fuel, energy, metal, cement and other materials become increasingly important. Any encroachment whatsoever that may occur on national prop-

[12] *Pravda,* 20 December, 1981.

erty must be decisively thwarted. We must with all the means and methods at our disposal close up all loopholes to parasitism, bribe-taking, speculation and other forms of unearned income.

The economy must be economical. This conclusion was confirmed by the XXVIth Congress of the CPSU as one of the most important principles of the Party's economic strategy at the present stage of our society's development. Concrete ways of solving questions connected with the raising of re-investments, the maximum capacity for equipment, information to a minimum of losses of energy, fuel, raw material and materials are defined by the June (1981) resolution of the Central Committee of the CPSU and USSR Council of Ministers. It envisages carrying out a system of measures aimed at the basic improvement of all work on the saving and rational use of resources. Strict observance of a procedure of economy is the common concern of all our people.

The Soviet people are approaching the solution to the problems before their country in a business-like way, with interest and a sense of responsibility. Socialist competition serves as the clearest example of such an approach, and of the patriotism of the working masses. More than 100 million people participate in it—all battling to put the resolutions of the XXVIth Party Congress successfully into practice with the slogan "Let us work efficiently and to a high standard!" The initiatives directed at the saving of material and labour resources and the output of high-quality products have been widely applied. A characteristic feature of socialist competition is its close link with the technological revolution. It concentrates all the more around the problems of the end results and the moral aspects of creative labour and the development of the individual.

The working man, his welfare and happiness are at the centre of the Party's plans and of the entire life of our developed socialist society. In the end, everything that we are planning to do in the eleventh five-year plan is subordinated to one purpose—the further raising of the people's welfare. It is only over the last three five-year plans that real income *per capita* of the population has doubled. All aspects of working people's lives are covered by the most important social measures. Some of these planned measures have already been put into practice in the first year of the current five-year plan. State aid to families with children has been increased and pensions improved. Since the XXVIth Congress of the CPSU the material situation of 4.5 million families with more than one child has been improved. 14 million pensioners have been given a supplement to their pensions. Workers in the coal industry are receiving increased pay.

The material benefits which the people of our country are getting from the Social Consumption Funds are continually increasing. 10-11 million Soviet people every year are celebrating housewarming parties. The network of nursery schools, schools, hospitals, clubs, libraries, cinemas, sanatoria-resort establishments and sporting facilities is expanding.

The Soviet people understand quite well that the all-round development of the country, the successful solution to current national economic problems as well as further improvements in living conditions can only be achieved by their own labour. They look upon the Party's plans as of deep concern to them; they work creatively and with initiative in all branches of communist construction, thus augmenting the economic and defence might of the socialist motherland.

3. The Leading Force of Soviet Society

The heroic past, glorious present and bright future of our country are continuously associated in the minds of Soviet people with the Communist Party, with its wise leadership. The most noble impulses of our hearts, the most profound feelings of the workers in town and country, and of the members of the armed forces all relate to the Party. They see in it the wisdom, honour and conscience of our age. The CPSU is building its whole revolutionary-transforming activity on the basis of the eternally living, constantly developing Marxist–Leninist doctrine. The Party embodies all that is best in the Soviet people—its revolutionary fighting spirit, unquenchable creative energy and capacity for work and wisdom. "The Communists are really the unbending core of our society, its living soul", said Comrade Brezhnev. "They are genuinely the revolutionary vanguard of the people."[13]

As the leading and guiding force in Soviet society, the Communist Party is growing, developing and becoming stronger together with it. Six and a half decades ago, in March 1917, it numbered 24,000 members. A 350,000-strong army of Bolshevik-Leninists were already spearheading the battle of the working class for the victory of the Great October Socialist Revolution. There are now nearly 18 million communists all sharing the same views and activities in the ranks of the CPSU. More than half of these are working directly in the area of material production—a key

[13] *Materials from the XXVIth Congress of the CPSU*, p. 218.

area of public life. Approximately 1.5 million primary and shop party organisations and party groups are conducting active daily tasks among the masses.

As the nucleus of the political system of Soviet society and of state and public organisations, the CPSU takes care of the all-round political leadership of state and public organisations and the creative activity of all the people. The Party channels the activities of state and public organs and organisations through the communists working in them and ensures that the efforts of all the links of the political system and national economic mechanism in communist construction are co-ordinated.

Almost a million deputy-communists are working in the Soviets of People's Deputies. They use their authority and experience to ensure that every session of the Soviet, every sitting of the permanent commissions, may turn into a real people's soviet, into a collective search for correct decisions.

The Soviet trade unions provide reliable support for the Party and are a powerful means for developing socialist democracy. Lenin's Komsomol[14] constitutes an active creative force. Many forms of democratic worker participation in the control of production, the speeding up of technological progress and solutions to socio-cultural and educational problems are generated by the creative work of the masses.

The CPSU fills the very important rôle of the Soviet people's vanguard in full accordance with the basic law of our state. It is written therein that all Party organisations are acting within the framework of the Soviet Constitution. The Party has never been a substitute for other organisations. On the contrary, it is invariably concerned that state and economic organs and public organisations should work with maximum efficiency and initiative and solve the problems before them creatively.

All the CPSU's leading and guiding activities are characterised by Lenin's style—a scientific, creative style that is alien to subjectivity, rules out complacency and opposes any form of red tape and formalism. The Central Committee of the CPSU, the Politburo of the Central Committee with its wide range of activities—the truly energetic headquarters of the Party—is an example of Lenin's style of leadership. "It is here", the XXVIth Congress of the CPSU observed, "that the collective intelligence of the Party comes together and forms Party policy expressing the interests of all Soviet society, of Communists and non-party people alike."[15]

[14] The Young Communist League.

[15] *Materials from the XXVIth Congress of the CPSU*, p. 69.

The purposeful and highly organised character of the work of the Politburo, the Central Committee and of the entire Party has been fashioned in large measure by Comrade Brezhnev's leadership of the Central Committee which lasted many years. Our country, the fraternal socialist countries and millions of people of good-will all over the world joyfully celebrated Comrade Brezhnev's 75th birthday. Expressing the thoughts and feelings of the communists in our country and of all the Soviet people, the Central Committee of the CPSU, the Praesidium of the USSR Supreme Soviet and the USSR Council of Ministers in their speech of welcome to Comrade Brezhnev noted his outstanding services applauding the truly invaluable contribution he had made in promoting the prosperity of our great country, the consolidation of its economic and defence might and the victory of the ideas of communism, peace and the social progress of mankind. As a stirring acknowledgement of these services, Comrade Brezhnev was awarded the Order of Lenin and the fourth Gold Star of Hero of the Soviet Union, as well as some high decorations from a number of other countries.

Our outstanding Party and state leader, the true continuer of Lenin's great cause, the acknowledged leader of today's revolutionary forces, Comrade Brezhnev enjoyed the boundless respect and love of the people. With his enormous capacity for work, his political perspicacity, his ability to keep cool and level-headed in the most critical situations and his benevolence, attention and sensitivity to people, Comrade Brezhnev created a healthy moral political atmosphere in the Party and country. Such an atmosphere promotes the increased public activity of the masses, their initiative and creativity and the flowering of talent which in our country, as Lenin said, is an inexhaustible spring. This enables the Party to solve the most complex problems successfully, to implement effectively the great mission of the leading power of society.

The very rich experience of our country and of the fraternal countries of socialism is convincing confirmation that the leadership of the Communist Party is essential and decisive for the successful construction and defence of the new society. It is not by chance that imperialist reaction and its underlings have spared no efforts and resources in their attempts to undermine and discredit the leading rôle of the Marxist–Leninist parties in the socialist countries and to belittle the importance of their rôle. These attempts are meant to weaken and shatter the very political foundations of socialism and to destroy the revolutionary gains of the workers. The Soviet people and peoples of the fraternal socialist countries are firmly and decisively repelling the intrigues of our class enemies and steadfastly following their communist vanguard.

The most important contribution to the development of socialist society is provided by the steadfast growth of the leading rôle of the Party. This contribution has a universal character. The increase in the range and complexity of problems to be solved and the intensification of activity in all links of the political system of socialist society demand that the level of organisational and political education work be steadily raised. And only the Communist Party—the political organisation equipped with Marxist–Leninist theory—can embrace the internal and external conditions of social development in its entirety, ensure effective leadership over the activity of the workers and work out correct policies and organise their practical implementation.

The CPSU is strong in its monolithic unity with the people. It is strong, as Lenin observed, because of its ability to communicate with, bring together and, to a certain extent, to blend with the mass of the workers. The inexhaustible vitality of CPSU policy is bound up with this. The Party has won the boundless trust and love of the people by its selfless service to them. The prestige of the CPSU is vast and indisputable. Many millions of people have become convinced of this through their own experience: the Party leads them along the only true path.

Of course, the rôle of the leading, guiding force in society is not just given it. As Comrade Brezhnev has observed, it "is earned, won in the course of the incessant struggle for the interests of the workers. And this rôle is strengthened in that the Party is constantly extending its connections with the masses, is alive to their needs and cares."[16]

The indestructible unity of Party and people is the invaluable property of our society. The unity of Party and people, forged and tempered by decades of revolutionary struggle and inspired creative work, which has passed through the toughest ordeals of the Civil War and the Great Patriotic War with honour, forms a durable foundation for the monolithic, ideological, social and international cohesion of Soviet society.

The ideological cohesion of our society is based on the communist world-outlook. It arms the Soviet people with a knowledge of the laws and perspectives of social development. Communist ideals, norms and principles are turned into convictions, determine the attitude of an individual to his social duty and the pattern of his daily behaviour and find concrete expression in the indissoluble unity of word and deed, in an important ac-

[16] *Materials from the XXVIth Congress of the CPSU*, pp. 218–219.

tive position and in moral integrity and purity. Communist conviction is a true compass which makes it possible to find one's correct bearings in any very complicated and critical situation and to recognise the class essence and direction in the intrigues of hostile ideology and to nip them firmly and decisively in the bud.

The Party has always seen and continues to see the goal of its programme as the forming of the new man, whose spiritual outlook is distinguished by communist conviction. With this in mind, the Party is working on a wide front, taking advantage of the opportunities provided by a mature socialist society and the entire very rich arsenal of organisational, political and educational means.

The most important place in the education of the Soviet people belongs to the study of Marxist–Leninist theory which under the conditions of developed socialism has become massive. Almost 23 million people are now involved in the system of Party education alone. The conducting of political education has been put into practice everywhere. By tirelessly striving to raise the level of Party education, the CPSU is seeking to teach the people, by Lenin's definition, "to act as communism would indeed require them to."[17]

The mass information media play a huge rôle in forming the social consciousness of the Soviet people and in further strengthening their ideological cohesion. Effective use of the media is instrumental in raising the level of knowledge, erudition and spiritual needs of the Soviet people.

Firmly based on socioeconomic reforms, and under the determining influence of the Party's Marxist–Leninist ideology and politics, the social cohesion of Soviet society is strengthened, the consistent trends towards integration of all its classes and social groups and its indissoluble union further strengthened. Comrade Brezhnev, when evaluating the development of Soviet society over the last few decades at the XXVIth Congress of the CPSU, put forward the thesis that "the coming into being of a classless society will mainly and basically occur within the historical framework of mature socialism".[18]

Implementation of the plans outlined by the Party for socioeconomic and cultural development will lead to the steady growth of the social homogeneity of our society. The working class, the collective farm peasantry and the intelligentsia are united in our country by common interests

[17] V.I. Lenin, *Poln. sobr. soch.*, vol. 41, p. 302.

[18] *Materials from the XXVIth Congress of the CPSU*, p. 53.

and ideals, by the relationships of collectivism, comradely co-operation and mutual aid. The social cohesion of Soviet society is being further consolidated in proportion to the growth in the education, culture and professional training of the widest sectors of workers. The gradual conversion of agricultural labour into a variety of industrial jobs, the erasing of social distinctions between workers in the industrial and agricultural sectors of the economy and the equalising of the material and daily cultural living conditions of town and village are playing a large part in this.

Advance along the road to communism is accompanied by reinforcement of the international cohesion of our society. The mighty brotherhood of more than 100 nations and nationalities which united six decades ago into one allied socialist state—the USSR— is full of inexhaustible vital forces. Their source is the Leninist national policy of the CPSU. By increasing the material and spiritual potential of each republic and at the same time by making the most of it for the harmonious development of the whole country, the achievements of the Soviet people under Party leadership have been truly historic. The most important changes in the economic, social and cultural life of Soviet society, in the life of all the peoples of the country and the profound democracy of our multi-national state have been given expression in the new Constitution of the USSR and the new constitution of the allied republics.

The Party sees it as its sacred duty to educate the working people in the spirit of Soviet patriotism and socialist internationalism and in the proud sense of identity with one great Soviet motherland. The experience of creating a new society and its defence in wartime and the very rich revolutionary practical work are convincing confirmation of the fact that one cannot be a patriot without being an internationalist. And the reverse—one cannot be an internationalist without being a patriot of the socialist fatherland. The unity of fundamental interests, creative tasks and historical fates of all the Soviet peoples makes our society even more cohesive and powerful.

When working out its political course and general future programme for communist construction, the Party is constantly studying and taking into full consideration the interests of all classes and social groups, of all the nations and nationalities of the USSR. It combines revolutionary theory with daily practice and finds support in the elevated social activity and political creativity of the masses. It is in this way that the truly national character of the CPSU's organising and guiding activities is formed. Embodying, as Comrade Brezhnev has observed, the collective intelligence of the best sons and daughters of a great people, the Party scientifically expresses in its policy what the people are conscious of, what best serves the needs of the socioeconomic development of the country and its dynamic advance along the road to communism.

It is just these all-round, well-grounded qualities, this political acumen and realism that characterise the resolutions of the XXVIth Congress of the CPSU. In struggling to put them into practice, the Soviet people are displaying great activity in their politics and work. The common cause of building communism, the common concern for strengthening the economic and defensive might of our country and the positions of world socialism, and the concern for securing peace and international security unite the Soviet people ever more closely round the Communist Party. The insuperable strength of the CPSU stems from its indestructible unity with the people. The mighty, invincible strength of the Soviet people stems from its unity with the Party.

2

The Cause of the Party, the Cause of All the People

1. The Defence of Socialism's Gains as an Objective Necessity

In concentrating their efforts in two interrelated directions—that of building communism and consolidating peace—the CPSU and the Soviet people are giving their unremitting attention to ensuring the security of the state and the reliable defence of socialist gains.

The defence of the revolutionary gains of the working people is an objective necessity. "No revolution", said Lenin, 'is of any value unless it can defend itself . . ."[1] Until the threat to the gains of socialism is contained, Lenin observed, our steps towards peace must be accompanied by full military preparedness, we must be on the *qui vive,* and look after the defence capability of our country and our Red Army as the apple of our eye.[2]

The Communist Party has consistently been guided and is still being guided by these instructions of Lenin at all stages in the development of the Soviet state. It organised, headed and ensured the victory of the young Red Army in its struggle against the forces involved in the foreign military intervention and internal counter-revolution who were attempting to smother the Socialist Revolution while still in the cradle. It urgently strengthened the military might of the Soviet armed forces in the twenties and thirties when imperialist reaction was engaged in massive preparation

[1] V.I. Lenin, *Poln. sobr. soch.,* vol. 37, p. 122.
[2] See V.I. Lenin, *Poln. sobr. soch.,* vol. 40, p. 248; vol. 44, p. 300.

for new aggression against the USSR. It organised and inspired the historic victory of the Soviet people and its armed forces in the Great Patriotic War.

The heroic history of our socialist motherland graphically confirms the indisputable truth that there is no force in the world that can topple socialism and conquer a people who are conscious of being masters of their country and who regard its defence as their own vital affair.

The lessons that the Soviet people have more than once taught aggressors who have dared to encroach on their land have not yet been learnt. Seekers of military adventures and the reactionary circles of imperialism have not relinquished their fantastic plans for crushing socialism by force of arms. Such plans have been elaborated in the USA already at the end of the forties and in the fifties. They were gambling on a sudden attack on the USSR using nuclear arms. And it was only the lofty military might of the Soviet armed forces and our own nuclear arms which had been manufactured in answer to US blackmail that held the United States back from aggression.

But designs for achieving military superiority over us and with it for untying their hands to conduct a global policy of *diktat* and piracy as before do not allow the warlike forces of imperialism any peace. These powers regard the Soviet Union and other countries of the socialist community as the chief obstacle to restoration of the international positions lost by imperialism. They strive in whatever way they can to hamper the consolidation of real socialism and to weaken and crush national liberation struggles and the world communism and working-class movement.

In the policy of imperialism today, certain traits stand out ever more nakedly such as adventurism and the readiness to gamble with the vital interests of mankind in the name of their own narrow and selfish aims. "Never, since the Second World War, has the situation been so serious".[3] Comrade Brezhnev observed. Wheresoever a reactionary régime foisted on the people may happen to fall apart at the seams, the forces of imperialism immediately make for it, the Americans first of all, to claim with fire and sword the "order" that is so dear to the monopolistic bourgeoisie and to defend the "vital interests" of those circles that make a fortune from exploiting other countries and peoples and from robbing them of their national wealth.

One of the clearest indicators of mounting imperialist aggression is provided by the unprecedented growth in its military preparations. The military budget of the USA and of other NATO countries is growing from

[3] *Pravda*, 4 February, 1982.

year to year. For example, in 1982 US expenditure amounted to 225 milliard dollars and in the projected budget for 1983 it exceeds 263 milliard dollars. During the present five-year plan (up till 1986), the US military budget will reach 1.5 trillion dollars, that is a sum which at current prices is six times higher than US military expenditure for the whole of the Second World War.

These allocations are destined, so we are told by US leaders, for maintenance of "the most powerful and flexible of armed forces", for the attainment of military superiority over the Soviet Union and other socialist countries. A new unprecedented programme for increasing stategic nuclear strength has also been declared in the USA. The deployment of the next generation of nuclear and conventional weapons is being accelerated. New types of weapons of mass destruction, chemical and bacteriological included, are being made. Production of the neutron bomb is to be on a large scale, and its adoption as an armament will lead to the creation of a new, refined method of unleashing nuclear war.

Following in the wake of America's aggressive policy, its NATO partners, Britain, the Federal German Republic and other countries are speeding up their military preparations. Thus, the direct military expenditure of all the member countries of the North Atlantic bloc has increased from 104 milliard dollars in 1970 to 254 milliard dollars in 1980. This expenditure exceeded 1.6 trillion dollars over the last ten years and continues to grow.

Widespread deliveries to troops of new tanks, planes, artillery and other weapons are being effected. The strategic reserves of NATO are on the increase and intensive measures are being put in hand to increase mobilisation possibilities and to improve the bloc's infrastructure. The allied armed forces of NATO in Europe number more than 3 million. This figure rises to almost 5 million for the total strength of the armies of the NATO countries.

NATO's plan for "arming up" with nuclear missiles is especially dangerous for the cause of peace. This envisages the additional deployment in Western Europe of around 600 new American medium-range missiles. If this were effected NATO would have a strength of one and a half times of that of the USSR in delivery vehicles and roughly double in nuclear warheads. As a consequence of this, not only would the existing balance in Europe be upset but also the balance of the strategic forces of the USSR and USA, and a qualitatively new military strategic situation would arise. The point is that the American missiles would be targetted on strategic objectives on Soviet territory and could be used as first-strike weapons. This would pose a serious threat to the security of the USSR and its allies.

Naturally, the Soviet Union cannot remain indifferent to such a prospect. It will not, as the XXVIth Congress of the CPSU emphasised with all certainty, allow a change in the existing parity of strength in favour of the USA and NATO. Our position in this matter is clear and unequivocal. It is based on strict observance of the principle of parity and equal security for all sides.

This principle is a real platform from which to solve all problems connected with military confrontation in Europe. However, despite this, ever newer, more sweeping plans are being made and put into operation for modernisation of the weaponry. The attacking potential of the army of the Federal German Republic is growing particularly fast, primarily as a result of a sharp increase in the number of tanks. The Bundeswehr has become NATO's chief striking force in Europe. The build-up of West German naval strength, which includes submarines, is being accelerated. The FRG has in fact been converted into an arsenal for American nuclear weapons. Such a large quantity of these weapons have been accommodated on her territory that their density is higher than in any other region of the world. All this is hardly evidence of NATO's peaceableness as the West tries to represent the matter.

The increased aggression of imperialism finds expression in the intensified activity of its bloc strategy. A tendency to expand NATO's functions and spheres of activity can be seen ever more clearly. The exercises and manoeuvres which are being conducted in NATO essentially constitute rehearsals for unleashing and conducting war against the Soviet Union and the other countries of the socialist community.

In addition to existing imperialistic military-political alliances, the USA is trying to create new ones, in particular the Pacific Community, the South Atlantic, Near Eastern and other military blocs. Ignoring the lessons of its own history, the United States is encouraging the revival of Japanese militarism. While trying to get round Washington, the imperialist forces of Japan are increasing military preparations in contravention of their country's Constitution. The campaign they have unleashed regarding territorial claims on the USSR is of a blatantly hostile, anti-Soviet character. At the same time Tokyo, within the framework of the Japanese–American "Mutual Security Treaty", is increasing its contributions to the US's military-strategic efforts in East Asia and the Pacific area.

Peking is taking up the rôle of active accomplice to the most warlike forces of imperialism. It is intensifying its efforts to bring the USA and NATO into conflict with the Soviet Union and other Warsaw Pact countries and is committing subversive, aggressive acts against neighbouring countries, in the first place against Vietnam, Laos and Kampuchea.

The incursion of Chinese forces into socialist Vietnam in February–March 1979 revealed the real face of the Peking rulers and the extent of the danger lurking behind their aggressive, adventurist policies. Chinese provocation against Vietnam and its threatening behaviour towards Laos and Kampuchea have not yet ceased. As a friend of Washington, Peking is participating in the undeclared war against Afghanistan.

The USA, a number of other NATO countries and Japan, who are counting on turning Peking's hostility towards the Soviet Union and the entire socialist community to good account, are strengthening their military and political ties with China. The decision of the US administration to sell modern weapons, some of them offensive, to Peking constitutes a special danger. A strategic alliance between American imperialism and Peking hegemonism is being knocked together behind the backs of the Chinese and American peoples.

The ominous growth of imperialist aggression can be followed in US efforts to expand and improve a network of military bases and establishments, primarily arranged around the USSR and other socialist countries. Washington is showing a feverish activity in the Near and Middle East. The construction of military bases is going on in Israel and Egypt, in the Oman and Saudi Arabia and old bases are being reconstructed in Bahrein, Kenya and Somalia. In Africa and the Arabian Peninsula the USA is making depots for tanks, artillery and other *matériel*, destined for a "rapid deployment force". The backbone of this force in the region must be the American forces who will be deployed in Sinai in accordance with the American–Israeli–Egyptian deal on the so-called multinational peacekeeping forces on the Sinai peninsula. Under the pretext of defending the "vital interests" of the USA in the Mediterranean, large contingents of American forces have been assembled there. And in the Indian Ocean two US aircraft carrier groups are stationed, for all intents and purposes on a permanent basis. Pakistan is gradually being converted into a major Pentagon base in Southwest Asia.

The USA is essentially striving to assert its military presence in the whole world. At the present time there are more than 1500 American military bases and establishments to be found in 32 countries. These are bases of aggression at which more than half a million US military personnel are concentrated. Hence, the American imperialist threat to the security of peoples.

The threat to peace posed by American military bases and establishments is all the greater in that the USA is equipping the forces in them not only with the most up-to-date weapons and conventional *matériel* but also with nuclear weapons. Thus more than seven thousand nuclear ammunition depots have been built at American military bases in Western Europe; approximately 1500 are situated in the Pacific Ocean zone, and more than 7,000 on ships and floating bases of America's Atlantic and Pacific fleets.

The danger is compounded by the fact that the American military bases are virtually outside the control of local authorities and the nuclear weapons accommodated there can be used without the knowledge and agreement of these authorities. This situation not only flouts the sovereignty of the countries concerned, but it turns them into the nuclear hostages of the United States.

American imperialism is making intense efforts to expand the centres of tension and to kindle armed conflict. Washington is behind all this and is essentially a direct accomplice in the escalation of Israel's aggressive actions. It is fanning the explosive situation in the Middle East, directing the expansionist policy of the Israeli aggressors and backing them up in every way possible within the framework of so-called "strategic co-operation". The scale of the threat with which the Middle Eastern centre of tension is fraught far exceeds the bounds of the region as far as the presence of nuclear potential in Israel is concerned; this is passed off by Washington as an "uncontrollable element". And this means that armed conflict here could change into nuclear conflict.

The United States interferes in the domestic affairs of sovereign states in almost every area of the world. It is equipping the bands invading Afghanistan on an increasing scale. Because of its direct complicity, the South African racists are behaving like brigands. The intrigues of American imperialism in Latin America are still continuing. The USA is keeping the anti-democratic, tyrannical régimes in El Salvador and Chile in money and arms. Washington does not spare means to activate struggles against national liberation movements in this area. At the same time, it is applying ever increasing military pressure on socialist Cuba. The USA is working up tension on absolutely groundless pretexts around "The Isle of Freedom" and is threatening it directly with "punitive action". The USA is grossly interfering in socialist Poland's domestic affairs.

The USA has lately been using the methods of international terrorism on a wider scale and is making attempts to regenerate the "big stick" policy rejected by the people, but now in the nuclear version. In accordance with this, a 200,000 "rapid deployment force" is being drawn up, various military resources are being taken in hand in good time, including nuclear weapons, on frontiers of forward-based forces in Western Europe, Asia and Africa. Leaders in the American administration are making no secret of the fact that the USA is prepared to use the neutron bomb in local wars.

The intensity of US aggression shows up in concentrated form in its military strategic conceptions. In Washington's proclamation of "a new nuclear strategy" the basic stake of the USA on a "pre-emptive surprise" nuclear strike against the Soviet Union and other countries of the socialist community is clearly expressed. Discussions are in full swing across the Atlantic on the permissibility of a so-called "limited" nuclear war and the chances of success "with a potential of assured destruction in readiness". They want to school the people of the Western countries to the criminal idea that it is acceptable to use nuclear weapons, and at the same time to blunt their vigilance.

There can simply be no "limited" nuclear war. This, as Comrade Brezhnev emphasised at the XXVIth Congress of the CPSU, is straightforward deception. Should US imperialism unleash a nuclear war, for example in Europe, it would from the very beginning lead to irreplaceable losses and the most fatal consequences for the countries situated there and to the destruction of entire peoples and their age-old civilisations. Moreover, it would inevitably and irrevocably acquire a world-wide character. That is why the calculations of those who hope to kindle a nuclear conflagration and to contain it within Europe, but at the same time to stand aside from the flames themselves and to expose their allies to a devastating retaliatory strike, is as cynical as it is illusory. Comrade Brezhnev emphasised that "the only sort of person who could start a nuclear war in the hope of winning it would be someone who had decided to commit suicide. Whatever power the attacker might possess, whatever method he might choose for unleashing nuclear war, he would not achieve his goals. Retribution would inevitably follow."[4]

At the same time as it is working out different ways of unleashing and conducting nuclear war, Washington is providing for the possibility of "a protracted conventional war" in various parts of the world. Such a war in the thinking of the Pentagon strategists would not in any way exclude nuclear war; on the contrary, it may serve as a sort of supplement to it. The leaders of the US Defense Department have declared more than once that the USA must be prepared to unleash and at the same time to conduct

[4] *Pravda,* 21 October, 1981.

large-scale and so-called "minor" wars in different parts of the globe. For example, the Pentagon is drawing up plans for conducting a "small" war in the Persian Gulf area envisaging the use of both conventional and nuclear weapons.

The content, character and trend of imperialism's aggressive conceptions and actions, with America in the forefront, show that in pursuance of its global aims it is, to all intents and purposes, hastening the demise of *détente* and exacerbating tension and the likelihood of confrontation. Lovers of military adventure should not forget that the Soviet Union has at its disposal enough strength and resources to protect its vital interests from any encroachments. If it should be necessary, the Soviet people, as Comrade Brezhnev observed, "will find ways to make additional efforts, to do all that is necessary to ensure the reliable defence of their country".[5]

The Soviet Union proceeds from the assumption that preservation of the existing parity, a consistent reduction of the likelihood of military confrontation and the reduction of armed strength and armaments with guarantees of equal security for all parties are basic criteria for the consolidation of peace. To count on victory in the arms race and especially in nuclear war is madness. And madness is dangerous. We do not need military superiority over the West. We only need reliable security and to ensure this it is enough to have a rough balance and parity. This is the unchanging approach of the USSR to this question. And the threadbare myth about the "Soviet military threat" that is forcing the West to arm itself is being circulated ever more intensively by imperialist propaganda as a smoke screen to cover up the aggressive aims of the USA and NATO. This is convincingly shown, for example, in the book published in our country at the beginning of 1982 entitled *Whence the Threat to Peace*. The myth about "the Soviet military threat" is circulated for the benefit of those who are growing rich on the arms race, to back the massive ideological preparation for aggression, and so delude international public opinion and to take the punch out of statements against the militaristic plans of the USA and NATO.

Keen vigilance today is especially essential in regard to the intrigues of the forces of international reaction and aggression. These forces are in possession of powerful up-to-date means of attacks, huge economic, technological and military potential and an abundance of manpower and natural resources. Their aggressive preparations and wild military strategic conceptions and plans represent a real threat to universal peace.

The Soviet Union and other countries of the socialist community are

[5] *Pravda*, 3 November, 1981.

opposing this threat with a firm and consistent struggle for peace, the security of peoples and social progress, and are in constant readiness to effectively rebuff any aggression. They are doing all they can to ensure peaceful conditions favourable for building the new society and to defend the gains of socialism with reliability all over the world. This objectively meets the basic interests of the Soviet people, the peoples of other socialist countries and of all humanity.

2. The Nationwide Character of Defence of the Socialist Fatherland

In its content, goals and tasks the defence of the socialist fatherland has a really nationwide character. Lenin saw the inexhaustible source of the stability of the system and of the might of the new socialist-type army in the dissoluble connection between the defence of the socialist state and the fundamental vital interests of the broad working masses. "Never," he pointed out, "will a people be conquered in whom the workers and peasants in their majority have recognised, felt and seen that they are defending their own Soviet power—the power of the working people who are defending a cause, the victory of which ensures for them and their children the chance of enjoying all the blessings of culture and all the creations of man's labour."[6]

All the multi-faceted activities of the Communist Party and the Soviet state concerned with the security of the USSR and of its allies and friends are built on the stable foundation of Lenin's teaching on the defence of the socialist fatherland. Guided by this teaching, the CPSU is developing it creatively in application to specific, historical conditions.

The nationwide character of the defence of the socialist fatherland can be seen most fully in wartime when the people rise up to ward off aggression and rout the enemy. The action of the forces on the battlefields and the intensive work of those toiling on the home front to provide the army with essentials flows together into one mighty current of national struggle for the attainment of victory.

Even at the dawn of Soviet power under the incredibly complex and difficult conditions of foreign military intervention and civil war, the working class, the broad masses of workers in our country, displayed under the leadership of the Bolshevik Party, as Lenin observed, the most serious attitude to the defence of the Republic of Soviets and an unexampled,

[6] V.I. Lenin, *Poln. sobr. soch.*, vol. 38, p. 315.

truly great heroism. When summing up the results of this struggle, Lenin emphasised that they had brought a greater mass of people to a conscious attitude to war and to active help in it than had ever been known before. The reasons for the final defeat of a strong enemy were based on this.

The Great Patriotic War embodied most clearly the national character of the defence of socialism. Our whole vast country was converted into one military camp united around the Communist Party as the organiser and inspirer of the Soviet people's selfless struggle at the front and elsewhere. The Soviet troops, drawing on the undivided support of the people, courageously and skilfully routed the hated enemy. Their staunchness, courage and self-sacrifice gave new strength to those who worked without sparing themselves on the home front, providing the armed forces with all the essentials for routing the enemy. This was a patriotic feat, the equal of which history has never known.

Our victories in the wars against imperialist aggressors and their numerous armies, which were equipped with the latest equipment and *matériel*, demonstrated to the whole world the might and invincibility of the socialist social and state system and the indisputable advantages of socialist military organisation over that of the capitalist. A modern world war, should imperialism manage to unleash it, would be incomparably more destructive than any past war, an ordeal for the army and people, with an unprecedented strain on all the material and spiritual resources of the country. This demands the timely and comprehensive preparation of the socialist state and all the people to ward off aggression.

The Soviet people understand this well. There is nothing dearer to them than the freedom, independence and happiness of their own country. They give of their labour, energy and talent to augment its wealth and prestige. They look upon its defence as a matter of concern to all of them. It is for this reason that the defensive might of the socialist state is indestructible.

What Lenin said about the impossibility of conducting a modern war against imperialism without serious economic preparation is as topical now as ever it was.[7] The Communist Party and the Soviet state, in organising and guiding the creative activity of the working masses, concentrate their main efforts on economic development, the highest goal of which is to raise steadily the standard of living. At the same time they are giving their unremitting attention to strengthening the country's defence and are doing everything necessary to satisfy its needs in full.

The successful solution of increasingly complex defence tasks is guaran-

[7] See V.I. Lenin, *Poln. sobr. soch.*, vol. 35, p. 390.

teed by the economic and technological potential created in our country. In developing and augmenting it, the Soviet people are attaining by their selfless labour a steady increase in the level of national welfare and the consistent strengthening of the material bases of the country's defence capability, the fighting efficiency of the armed forces.

In whatever area of communist construction Soviet man may be working, he is contributing his mite to strengthening his country's power and is in some way or other participating in the solution of problems connected with its defence. The worker and collective farmer, the engineer and technician, the scientist and designer—every citizen of the Soviet Union—regards his own personal interests and fate as inextricably bound up with the interests and fortunes of his country. All the defensive measures of the Party and State draw on the unanimous support, the inexhaustible initiative and creativity of the Soviet people.

The national character of the defence of the socialist fatherland finds expression in the steady strengthening of the sociopolitical foundations of the country's defence capability, the fighting might of the armed forces. This is a result in keeping with the merging of fundamental interests and the close co-operation of all classes and social groups, nations and nationalities of our country in one great cause—the construction of communism and the defence of the fatherland. The entire Soviet people—the new historic community of people—now constitutes the base of the armed forces.

The defence of the socialist fatherland is defined by our Constitution as the sacred duty of every Soviet citizen. And the Soviet people fulfil this duty with merit and honour. In accordance with the law of the USSR on universal military duty they serve in the ranks of the armed forces, thus taking direct part in the solution to the country's defence problems. Workers in the towns and villages actively participate in state defence measures. Families, schools, working collectives, trade unions and other public organisations make their contribution to the cause of defence.

The Leninist Komsomol plays a large part in inculcating Soviet youth and personnel of the armed forces in lofty moral and political qualities. This rôle is all the more important in view of the fact that young people constitute three-quarters of the personnel of the armed forces. Under communist leadership the Komsomol organisations participate daily in educating troops, who are politically active, thoroughly familiar with military matters, boundlessly devoted to the Party and people and always ready to defend their country.

The Voluntary Society for Collaboration with the Soviet Army, Airforce and Navy[8] is carrying out a huge job in mass defence. More than one-third of those called up receive good training in their educational institutions and study special subjects essential to the armed forces and the economy. The Voluntary Association for Collaboration with the Army, Navy and Airforce of the USSR rightly calls it the preparatory class for that big school of life, i.e. service in the ranks of the armed forces.

The continual consolidation of the moral foundations of the country's defence capability and of the fighting efficiency of the armed forces lends a new dimension to the national character of Soviet defence. Developed socialism provides especially favourable conditions for the growth of ideological maturity, the broadening of political horizons, the raising of the general cultural level and social activity of Soviet citizens, including army, navy and airforce personnel.

Soviet society is, as the XXVIth Congress of the CPSU remarked, a society of working people. Creative, enterprising labour increasingly becomes the first vital need of every Soviet person. Military service gives wide scope for initiative. Our troops are constantly raising their ideological level, mastering modern weapons and *matériel*, becoming physically tougher, striving more fully to fulfil their educational plans and programmes and all the tasks which the Party and people are setting the armed forces.

The monolithic sociopolitical and ideological unity of the Soviet people gives the armed forces invincible might and constantly nourishes their unwavering devotion to the Party, the country and the high ideals of communism. The indissoluble community of interests, goals and ideals and the merging of the patriotic and international efforts of urban and rural workers and of army, navy and airforce personnel, is a guarantee of the further growth of the fighting power and preparedness of the Soviet armed forces, and of the reliable defence of socialism's gains throughout the world.

3. CPSU Leadership—the Very Basis of Soviet Military Organisation

The national concern for strengthening the country's defence, perfecting the armed forces and guaranteeing peaceful conditions for communist construction finds expression in Communist Party policy and in its daily

[8] The initial letters in Russian are DOSAAF.

guidance of military organisation. The Party works out military policy, which includes technological matters and military doctrine, guides the daily life and activities of the army, navy and airforce and directs the development of Soviet military science and skill, and the training and education of military cadres and all personnel. It also organises work which aims to increase military preparedness and to develop international ties with the armies of the fraternal socialist countries and to strengthen military co-operation with them.

The solving of political, economic, social and ideological tasks is closely linked with the Party's organisation and guidance of armed forces development. Lenin pointed out the exceptional importance of such an interrelationship. He emphasised that the development of our armed forces can only bring successful results if it is carried out in the same spirit as that of general Soviet construction.[9]

The principle of the Party to strengthen the defence capability of the country, to develop and improve the military organisation of socialist society, was, on Lenin's initiative, formulated in the resolution of the Party's Central Committee of 25 December 1918. ". . . The policy of the War Department, as of all other departments and institutions," the resolution noted, "is conducted on the precise basis of the general directives issued by the Party's Central Committee and under its direct control."[10] This position has been strengthened in the programme of the CPSU in which it is emphasised that the Communist Party's guidance of the armed forces and the reinforcement of the rôle and influence of Party organisations in the armed forces is the very basis of armed forces development.[11]

The Party's guidance of military organisation covers all spheres connected with the strengthening of the country's defence capability and the raising of military preparedness. The working out of military policy is the most important of these. This process is based on continuous, all-round analysis, objective evaluation and correct assessment of the world political situation and of the particular characteristics and tendencies of the country's socioeconomic development. Lenin pointed out the great importance of specific analysis for a specific situation.[12]

Soviet military policy is a component part of the whole policy of the Party and State. Its high standard of efficiency is achieved by uniting political, economic and military leadership. It is imbued with the ideas

[9] See V.I. Lenin, *Poln. sobr. soch.*, vol. 40, pp. 76–77.

[10] *The CPSU on the Armed Forces of the Soviet Union: Documents 1917–1981*, Moscow, 1981, p. 42.

[11] *Programme of the CPSU*, Moscow, 1976, p. 112.

[12] See V.I. Lenin, *Poln. sobr. soch.*, vol. 41, p. 136.

contained in Lenin's teaching on the defence of the socialist fatherland and with a spirit of proletarian, socialist internationalism and is inextricably bound up with the consistent peace policy pursued by the CPSU in the international arena. "Devotion to the cause of peace and peaceful co-operation with other countries," Comrade Brezhnev remarked, "is determined by the very character of our society. This is why we do not have and will not have advocates of war, aggression and adventurism in politics."[13]

The equitable goals of our peace policy in the international arena find reflection in Soviet doctrine. Its content is much drawn upon for fulfilling tasks involving the defence of socialist gains, the peaceable work of the Soviet people, the sovereignty and territorial integrity of the USSR and the security of our friends and allies. This was revealed with the utmost clarity in an interview given by Comrade Brezhnev to the periodical *Der Spiegel*. "The Soviet Union," he emphasised, "poses no threat to anyone, does not intend to attack anyone. And our military policy is of a defensive nature. It rules out preventive wars and the idea of 'a first strike'."[14]

In their attempts to distort the essential quality of Soviet military doctrine, Western politicians and strategists ascribe expansionist features to it. The ill-intentioned nature of such assertions is obvious. The orientation quality of a military doctrine depends wholly on the class nature of the state and its policy. Aggressive, expansionist aims are alien to the Soviet socialist state. Its domestic policy is one of peace, friendship and co-operation between peoples. The defensive orientation of Soviet military doctrine invariably flows from this. The USSR has always opposed and continues to oppose the idea of the so-called "first disarming strike", and the "limited", as indeed any other, nuclear war or similar wars. Our country's efforts are directed at not allowing either a first or any other strike, at averting nuclear war and eliminating the threat of its breaking out.

A most important place in the activities of the Communist Party in guiding armed forces development is filled by daily organisational work. It covers the development and reinforcement of the material and moral foundations of Soviet defence capability and the raising of the fighting power and preparedness of the Soviet armed forces. The CPSU directs the work of government bodies, public organisations and officials concerned with maintaining security and strengthening the country's defence capability. They guide the training, correct selection and placement in the army, navy and airforce of command, political, engineering and technical cadres and

[13] *Pravda,* 20 December, 1981.
[14] *Pravda,* 3 November, 1981.

ensure that the entire personnel makes skilful use of the materiotechnical base of the armed forces and of the resources designated to help in steadily increasing military preparedness.

The Party gives its constant attention to improving party political work in the army, navy and airforce and to giving Soviet troops an all-round education. It requires the military cadres to study very thoroughly the experience of the Great Patriotic War and the way it was handled. The further all-round development of co-operation in the sphere of defence with the fraternal socialist countries is the object of the CPSU's unremitting concern.

In today's conditions, the importance of the Party's guidance in armed forces development is steadily growing. This is conditioned by a whole string of factors.

First of all, there is the increasing complexity of tasks connected with defence of the socialist fatherland in the age of nuclear and other weapons of mass destruction. ". . . The character of modern weapons", Comrade Brezhnev emphasised, "has become such that were they to be used, the future of all mankind would be put at risk."[15] Never before has the task of averting war, curbing aggressors and maintaining peace been so critical. And never before has there been such a great responsibility on the part of the CPSU, as the ruling party, to ensure the country's safety, peaceful conditions for communist construction and the defence of socialist gains throughout the world.

The growth of the Party's rôle in guiding armed forces development is brought about by the quantitative changes taking place in the armed forces and in military matters as a whole. With the rapid development of science and technology new problems are arising in connection with the technical equipment of the armed forces and consequently with the planning, production, delivery and handling of modern armaments. This, in turn, demands new forms and methods of military activity, constant improvements in the organisational structure of the armed forces and in its training system and the development of scientific military thinking. And the Party as the ruling and guiding force in society is organising the solution to these problems by attracting the essential forces and resources.

The Party's increased rôle in guiding armed forces development is also brought about by the growing importance of the moral political factor in war. A modern war, especially a nuclear missile war, if the imperialists were to unleash it, would fundamentally change people's life-styles and would be

[15] *Pravda*, 24 June, 1981.

accompanied by unprecedented heavy psychological strain. The enormous scale, bitterness and intensity of hostilities would demand the greatest physical and moral effort from the personnel of the armed forces and all the people. Under these conditions the Communist Party, as always, would demonstrate the cementing and mobilising strength which forms the basis for the unbending staunchness of the masses and their determination to defeat the aggressor decisively. With their consistent, purposeful, ideological, political educational work the Party is continuously shaping in the minds of the Soviet people lofty moral and political qualities, the readiness and ability to withstand the huge burdens and deprivations of war and to carry out their duty to the very end with regard to defence of the socialist fatherland.

The rôle played by the Party in guiding armed forces development is becoming greater owing to the growing number of international tasks that the Soviet Union and its armed forces are taking on in connection with the defence of socialist gains. The volume of these tasks, the scale of the work on coordinating joint economic, political and military efforts with the other countries of the socialist community, has significantly increased and continues to do so. Common views on the character of modern warfare have to be worked out as do methods for conducting it; the organisation principles for structuring and improving the armed forces, and the content, forms and methods of instruction and education of personnel demand increasing attention. The vast revolutionary experience and very high international prestige of our Party and its consistent Leninist internationalist position which has gained the approval and support of all the fraternal parties is playing a most important part in successfully solving all these and many other problems.

In directing the country's defence and the life and activities of the armed forces on a daily basis, the CPSU takes all these factors into consideration and is continually improving its political, theoretical and organisational work. There is no aspect or area in armed forces development in which the Party's constant beneficial influence is not felt, as is also the influence of its Central Committee, the Politburo of the Central Committee and the General Secretary of the Central Committee of the CPSU, President of the Praesidium of the USSR Supreme Soviet, President of the USSR Defence Council, Marshal of the Soviet Union, the late Leonid Brezhnev. In his works and speeches and his exceptionally fruitful activity in guiding the Party and country we find the further creative development and practical embodiment of Lenin's ideas on the defence of the socialist fatherland, and the current problems of armed forces development receive thorough and detailed elaboration.

Comrade Brezhnev made an important contribution to developing the teaching on the guiding rôle of the Communist Party, including the area of defence, under conditions in which real socialism is no longer confined to one country and has created a basically new alignment of class forces in the international area. "Experience tells us," stressed Comrade Brezhnev, "that the victory of a socialist system in one country or other may only be regarded as conclusive in today's conditions, and a return to capitalism be ruled out, if the Communist Party, as the ruling force in society, firmly follows the Marxist–Leninist line by developing all the different areas of social life; only if the Party tirelessly reinforces the country's defence and protection of its revolutionary gains, if it instils and maintains vigilance in the people in relation to the class enemy, and irreconcilability to bourgeois ideology, only if the principle of socialist internationalism is faithfully observed and unity and fraternal solidarity with other Socialist countries strengthened."[16]

The outstanding victories of the Soviet armed forces over the enemies of the socialist fatherland and the present high standard of the armed forces visibly and convincingly confirm the decisive importance of CPSU guidance of armed forces development. There is, in this wise leadership, a reliable guarantee of the indestructible defensive might of the Soviet Union and the constant excellent fighting capacity and preparedness of its armed forces.

[16] L.I. Brezhnev, *Leninskim kursom,* vol. 2, pp. 329–330.

3

Keeping Watch over Peaceful Labour

1. The Armed Forces of the Socialist National State

Our armed forces have a great, truly heroic history. It has been made by all the generations of defenders of the socialist fatherland—from the Red Guards of 1917 to the troops of the eighties. And whatever page of history we may turn to, each one clearly testifies to the unwavering devotion of the Soviet troops to the people, the country and the great cause of the Party—the cause of communism.

During the unprecedented ordeals of the Civil War and the Great Patriotic War and in selfless efforts in war- and peacetime the armed forces have honourably justified and continue to justify their calling which consists, as Lenin defined, in protecting the gains of the Revolution, the power of the people and the entire new and truly democratic régime from all enemies.[1]

The fundamental, principal difference of the Soviet armed forces from the armies of the exploiter states who are anti-democratic by their class essence and political intention lies in this lofty calling. Apologists for imperialism try to represent the bourgeois armies as forces that are above class, that stand "outside politics" and serve "the whole nation". Lenin called such statements trite, hypocritical and false. They are especially convenient for covering up the intentions of the monopolistic bourgeoisie to use the army as its obedient tool in achieving anti-democratic aggressive aims.

[1] V.I. Lenin, *Poln. sobr. soch.*, vol. 35, p. 216.

As opposed to the bourgeois army, which by virtue of its class nature and intention is isolated from the people and opposed to working masses, the armed forces of the socialist state are an integral part of the people and share with them the same life, the same cares and interests. Their development and improvement is going on at the same time as that of the entire system of socialist social relations.

In the course of building a new society in our country and of perfecting socialist democracy and statehood, the Soviet armed forces have changed from an organ of the state of proletarian dictatorship to that of the state of the whole people. This necessity is conditioned by the military threat being posed by imperialist circles, but our fighting power is exclusively directed at defending the peaceable creative labour of the Soviet people and the great socialist gains from aggressors. Our armed forces are carrying out their lofty mission in unity with the armies of the other countries of the socialist community.

In the worsening international situation, the rôle and responsibility of the Soviet armed forces in guaranteeing the security of the USSR and of our friends and allies and in preserving peace on earth is greater than ever before. The escalation of imperialist aggression and of US and NATO military preparations directed against the USSR and other socialist countries require the Soviet armed forces to be maintained in a state of high military preparedness with improved equipment, organisational structure and forms and methods of training, instruction and education.

The present stage in the development of the armed forces is marked by a further improvement in the handling of weapons and *matériel* by personnel, by a steady increase in the field, air and naval training and the strengthening of organisation and discipline. The fighting co-ordination of formations, units and ships is also growing.

The remarkable sociopolitical features that characterise the armed forces and above all their stable sociopolitical unity find expression in the daily practical activity of the troops and in their patriotic accomplishments.

All Soviet troops—from the soldier to the marshal—are representatives of the friendly classes and social groups of our society. The sharing of social and class interests, of a scientific materialistic outlook and communist morality unites them. The attractive word *tovarishch* serves to symbolise the fighting unity of the troops of our armed forces; without this word the friendship of Soviet citizens in uniform is inconceivable. More than 90 per cent of the officers, ensigns, warrant officers, sergeants, sergeant-majors, petty officers and sailors are communists and Komsomol members. All Soviet troops regard each other as true fighting comrades who hand in hand carry out their sacred duty of defending the socialist fatherland.

The thorough-going process of establishing the classless structure of our developed socialist society gives particular strength to military collectives. Being naturally reflected in the development of the armed forces, this process fills military discipline with vital force, ensures the effectiveness of the combined command principle and makes it possible to achieve co-ordination and the merging of will and action in all personnel in the interests of resolving the problems faced by the armed forces. A commander's order is considered by subordinates as the country's command. Its precise and unquestioning execution corresponds in full to the inner convictions of the troops.

The indestructible sociopolitical unity of the Soviet troops determines their conscious attitude to their patriotic and international duty, serves as an inexhaustible source for the selfless execution of any, even the most difficult, tasks on the battlefield.

Our armed forces today are, as the Party envisaged they would be at its VIIIth Congress, "a *national* army in the real sense of the word . . .".[2] This finds expression in their socio-class and national structure, in their living, indivisible unity with the people. The armed forces' implementation of the tasks before them regarding the defence of the socialist fatherland stands out as an essential and important aspect of the national cause of building communism.

The direct participation of servicemen in the political, social and economic activity of the people acquires ever more varied forms. Servicemen are elected to the staff of leading Party and Soviet organs and worthily fulfil the duties imposed on them. The representatives of the armed forces do a great deal of work in public organisations and creative unions.

Quite a large amount of living accommodation and social and cultural establishments are erected by army builders. With their help a number of important national economic projects have been created and more than 1000 kilometres of surfaced roadway completed. The troops of the railway forces are helping to build a number of railways and are labouring on the eastern section of the Baikal–Amur line. Soviet troops contribute actively

[2] *CPSU in Resolutions and Decisions of Congresses, Conferences and Plenums of the Central Committee*, Moscow, 1970, vol. 2, p. 69.

to bringing in the harvest and solving other national economic tasks.

They play quite a considerable part in the country's athletic achievements. In fact, at the recent winter and summer Olympics army and navy sportsmen in combined Soviet teams came away with 45 gold, 47 silver and 29 bronze medals.

The varied sponsored associations between working and military collectives are stirring evidence of the close unity between the army and the people. Exchange visits, meetings, accounts of achievements at work and the fulfilment of socialist obligations, joint leisure evenings, amateur concert exchanges and other events are part of daily practice.

The manoeuvres and exercises carried out by the armed forces clearly demonstrate the close unity between the people and the army. The "West-81" exercises, for example, were accompanied by numerous displays of love and respect on the part of Soviet workers for their armed protectors. Everywhere that the troops and naval forces were operating, the population went out to meet them with much cordiality and warmth and extended care and attention to them.

Under the conditions of developed socialism that remarkable feature of the Soviet armed forces, the fraternal friendship between troops of different nationalities, stands out in ever greater relief. The sons of all the Soviet brother peoples live and serve side by side in army and navy collectives and carry out responsible tasks concerned with the defence of the socialist fatherland. "Our army," said Comrade Brezhnev, "is special in the sense that it is a school of internationalism, a school that teaches feelings of brotherhood, solidarity and mutual respect between all the nations and nationalities of the Soviet Union. Our armed forces are one friendly family, a living embodiment of socialist internationalism."[3]

A great feeling of patriotism is characteristic of army and navy troops as of all Soviet people. It is a feeling of national pride which motivates them to guard sacredly the honour and dignity of the armed protector of the socialist fatherland and to carry out their military service in an irreproachable fashion.

Communist thinking, political maturity and self-discipline in the troops, qualities which are an important feature of the armed forces, are making themselves more fully felt. This feature reflects the ideological political conviction, the moral strength and spiritual richness of the Soviet people. The socialist régime, Marxist–Leninist ideology, CPSU policy and our Soviet way of life provide the source for it.

[3] L.I. Brezhnev, *Leninskim kursom: rechi i stat'i, Moscow,* 1974, vol. 4, p. 61.

The Soviet fighting man is educated by the Party in high revolutionary ideals and in the tradition of selfless and wholehearted service to the socialist fatherland, in patriotism and internationalism. The working people of our country, the peoples of the fraternal socialist countries and all honest people everywhere see in him a man with a well-developed sense of duty and remarkable moral qualities. The Soviet fighting man has broad political vision, professional skill, an unbending will to victory over the enemy in battle, good sense of organisation and discipline, initiative and a creative approach to carrying out the tasks before him. In his person, communist ideology, genuine humanism, self-sacrifice, courage and a readiness to act in his country's name blend into one.

Describing today's fighting men at the XXVIth Congress, Comrade Brezhnev observed: "The sons and grandsons of heroes of the Great Patriotic War are now among those who defend the fatherland. They have not passed through the terrible ordeals that fell to the lot of their fathers and grandfathers but they are loyal to the heroic traditions of our army and people. And every time interests demand the country's security and the defence of peace and the victims of aggression need help, the Soviet fighting man stands before the world as a selfless and courageous patriot and internationalist ready to overcome any and all difficulties."[4]

The implementation of the Party line on the all-round, harmonious development of personality in Soviet man and the steady growth of the people's material and cultural standard of living is having its effect on the armed forces. The good, general training that the young people receive on entering the army and navy helps them to handle sophisticated weapons and *matériel* successfully in short periods of time, to learn the "secrets" of military skill and to develop themselves physically and spiritually.

In today's conditions, the importance of the beneficial, educational rôle of the Soviet armed forces is growing. This rôle is a distinguishing feature particularly of the socialist army which serves the people, the ideals of freedom, justice and humanitarianism, and protects the interests of the working people, the cause of peace and social progress. The content and trend of all personnel training is determined by this. Our armed forces are justly called a school of political, military and moral education, a school of courage, industriousness, collectivism, organisation and discipline.

The Communist Party and Soviet people value highly the educational rôle of the armed forces. Comrade Brezhnev talked about it with great warmth on many occasions. The high esteem in which he held it imposes

[4] *Materials of the XXVIth Congress of the CPSU*, p. 66.

great responsibility on the commanders, staff and political organs, the army and navy Party and Komsomol organisations and on all Soviet troops. They are called on all the time to keep steadily raising the educational rôle of the Soviet armed forces. This requirement flows directly from the resolution of the Central Committee of the CPSU "on the further improvement of ideological, political-educational work" and from the materials and decisions of the XXVIth Party Congress.

The need for and importance of a steady increase in the educational rôle of the armed forces are conditioned by many objective and subjective factors, first of all by the complexity of the problems being solved by the army and navy and the increased demands that have arisen on their military preparedness.

The importance of the educational influence of military service is determined by the fact that it represents an important stage in the life of practically every young person in our country. As far as time is concerned, this stage comes when the personality is undergoing its most intense moulding, when it is acquiring a civic and social sense. How many sergeants, petty officers, soldiers and sailors there must be who, on leaving the reserves, will keep these remarkable qualities acquired in the armed forces all their lives, and remember their school of military service with unchanging gratitude!

The armed forces have gained a large amount of experience in educational work. This experience shows that an indispensable condition for the success of this work is the thoughtful and thorough analysis and consideration of new phenomena and processes occurring in military matters, of changes in the technical equipment of forces, in personnel and in the content and character of military service. Consolidation of the material base, improvements in the educational process and the higher qualifications and teaching ability of the officers, political, engineering and technical staff make it possible to perfect the forms and methods of ideological and political educational work on a continuous basis. It is important to know how to make the best use of these educational opportunities of studies and training, flying and cruising, missile launchings and patrol duty. This study activity produces the best results if done in conditions simulating real hostilities. We must always remember the well-known truism: we must not teach without educating or educate without teaching.

It goes without saying that the educational rôle of the armed forces is not just confined to military service. The armed forces have an important, formative influence on the rising generation, on youth undergoing pre-conscription military training. They make a significant contribution to the patriotic military education of the country's entire population. Servicemen actively participate in the propagation of heroic fighting traditions, in giving the workers pride in the glorious past of our socialist fatherland and in the Soviet armed forces, and they help in forming constant vigilance with regard to the intrigues of imperialist aggressors. The officers, political organs, Party and Komsomol organisations of the army and navy give a great deal of help to local Party and Soviet organs, to the Leninist Young Communist League committees and to the Voluntary Association of Assistance to the Army, Airforce and Navy with the preparation and organisation of the all-Union military sporting games of "Zarnitsa" ("Summer Lightning") and "Orlenok" ("Eaglet"), with hiking tours for young people around places of revolutionary, military and labour fame and with the activities of a massive network of technical, shooting and other clubs and sections.

Of course not all the sociopolitical features of the Soviet armed forces are examined here but only those in which the historical destiny, socialist nature and national character are most graphically revealed.

Everything the fighting men of the armed forces do—the way they live, their work and aspirations—is inseparable from the lives and activities, the thoughts and aims of the Soviet people. Strong in their revolutionary fighting spirit, their unshakeable communist conviction and close unity around the Party, they selflessly and devotedly carry out their sacred duty to their country.

2. Keeping Abreast with Scientific and Technological Progress

Lenin saw the mutual reinforcement of the material and spiritual aspects of socialist military organisation as an indispensable condition for guaranteeing the reliable defence of the country and the high fighting power and military preparedness of the armed forces. Lenin pointed out that even the best army, even the people most devoted to the cause of revolution, would be immediately wiped out by the enemy if they were not sufficiently armed, supplied with food and trained.[5]

The character of military action, the scale, methods and forms of combat and operations and in the end the success in carrying out the tasks before the armed forces are largely determined by what weapons and

[5] V.I. Lenin, *Poln. sobr. soch.*, vol. 35, p. 408.

matériel they have at their disposal and how well provided for they are in the materiotechnical respect. Taking this into consideration, the Communist Party and the Soviet people, in fulfilling Lenin's behests, take unceasing care that our armed forces keep abreast of modern scientific and technological progress. Undoubtedly implementation of the national economic plans outlined by the XXVIth Congress of the CPSU will, together with this, promote further improvements in the technical equipment of the armed forces.

It is important to emphasise the following circumstances in this connection. The class essence and the use to which the achievements of technological progress in military development are put flow from the socioeconomic state system and its policies. These are diametrically opposite in socialist and imperialist countries.

There is a tendency inherent in imperialism for the influence of the military-industrial complex to grow steadily, for the militarisation of all aspects of life and the activity of bourgeois society to be reinforced—that is the home and foreign policies of the ruling class, of bourgeois ideology, science and culture. The best achievements of mankind's genius in the imperialist states are subordinated to the anti-democratic interests of monopoly; these interests strive to preserve capitalism at any price and to exploit the workers of their own country and the peoples of other countries. The imperialists see military strength as the chief tool for guaranteeing these interests. Drawing support from it, they conduct a policy of *diktat,* oppression and flagrant interference in the affairs of other states and peoples. The arms race being whipped up by imperialism serves to increase this military strength. Producing ever newer types of armament, the monopolies increase their profits. To prevent these profits from diminishing they do everything possible to step up international tension.

In the capitalist countries, above all in the USA, science is almost completely subordinated to militarism. The application of the very latest scientific and technological achievements is invariably turned against the workers, the cause of peace and social progress.

It is only the new social system of socialism that has placed the achievements of science and technology at the service of the people for the first time in history. In military affairs it uses these achievements in the interests of averting unjust, aggressive wars and to curb aggressors. In the Soviet Union and other countries of the socialist community there are no classes, social strata or groups who have an interest in war. Socialism by its very nature adheres to peace and considers constant concern over the working man's welfare and happiness as central to the life of society.

Our devotion to the cause of peace is consistent and unwavering. Far from ruling out, however, it presupposes the most attentive attitude to the country's defence. In order to ensure peaceful conditions for communist construction, we are reinforcing our defensive might. Here the development of events in the global arena and the peculiarities and tendencies of the international military political situation are being considered from all angles. In today's conditions, when the aggressive preparations of imperialism have appreciably increased and calculations for the achievement of military and technological superiority over the USSR can be seen ever more clearly in US strategic plans, we are compelled to maintain the equipment of our armed forces at a level which excludes the attainment of such superiority over us.

Proceeding from a thorough and realistic analysis of the international situation and taking into account the current state of military affairs and their future prospects, the Communist Party, on the basis of socioeconomic and technological achievements and the potentials of Soviet society, is working out and putting into practice a programme for the technological equipment of the armed forces which will ensure the rational and balanced development of all types of armament. Here special emphasis is being put on those weapons that play a definite rôle in increasing the preparedness of the armed forces in the event that they may have to fend off any possible aggression. The CPSU is directing the activities of scientific organisations and industry and is concentrating its efforts on longer-term problems, the solution of which, together with the implementation of current national economic tasks, will help to strengthen the country's defence.

The Soviet Union has experienced scientific cadres at its disposal and a well-developed network of scientific research institutions in all areas of knowledge. Our industries are in a position to turn out the most complex products including all sorts of new armaments. With these great possibilities for designing and producing up-to-date military equipment, the USSR is compelled to take necessary measures to ensure its security and the security of our allies in face of the growing military potential of the United States of America and its NATO partners. However it would not want to travel the path of competition in this sphere with anyone at all. Our position in this matter has been made clear many times in the documents of the Communist Party and the Soviet state, in the works and speeches of the former General Secretary of the Central Committee of the CPSU, the President of the Praesidium of the USSR Supreme Soviet, Comrade Brezhnev. "Peace based on mutual fear does not appeal to us," said Comrade Brezhnev. "We prefer a peace in which the level of armaments drops lower and lower, and the scale and quality of co-operation in all spheres grow and improve".[6]

In their attempts to attain military technological superiority over us, the US imperialist circles are staking most on strategic nuclear weapons. At the time, when the USA had the monopoly on atomic weapons, they counted on using this to blackmail peoples and states, to support a "world" order that suited Washington and to "push back" socialism.

The Soviet Union was faced with the necessity to liquidate this extremely dangerous US monopoly in the shortest possible time. We also made nuclear weapons. As matters were to prove later, this was a correct, far-sighted step. Nuclear weapons became a powerful shield which made the USSR, its state interests and the interests of the fraternal socialist countries secure. At the same time it moderated the ardour of the imperialist warmongers for a new war, for even after the barbarous bombing of Hiroshima and Nagasaki in August 1945 they had raised more than once the threat of an atom bomb over the world. If there had been no such weapons in our arsenal, the aggressive imperialist circles might have cast the world into the abyss of nuclear war long ago.

We have never striven and will never strive for superiority in nuclear weapons as we consistently stand for their limitation and complete prohibition. Only exceptional circumstances—direct nuclear aggression against the Soviet state or allies—can force us to resort to a retaliatory nuclear strike as an extreme method of self-defence.

In the struggle to avert a new war, we are also doing everything we can to prevent the aggressive imperialist circles from attaining superiority over the USSR in conventional weapons. Improvements are being made in the tactical and technical characteristics of our tanks, in artillery systems, mortars, planes and helicopters, ships and other kinds of armament and *matériel*. Their possibilities are being expanded, their power, range and accuracy, manoeuvrability, reliability and durability increased. Their fire and manoeuvre control are being automated. All this raises the efficiency of the weapons and the accuracy of hitting ground, air and sea targets.

The up-to-date level of science and technology makes it possible to solve problems on further qualitative improvements in armaments. But the new

[6] *Pravda*, 23 May, 1981.

weapons are essentially more difficult to use and make increased demands on the training of personnel. This also leads to significant organisational changes within the army and navy. Therefore Lenin's instruction that "it is impossible to build an up-to-date army without science"[7] is especially topical. And if our science as a whole is becoming increasingly a direct productive force, Soviet military science is becoming actively prominent as a major factor in improving the armed forces.

There is no doubt that however complex modern warfare may be, however dynamic, varied and at times contradictory its course, the development of military activity is, in the final count, determined by objective laws. Soviet military science is making a close study of these and searching for ways to use them skilfully. The correctness of its principal positions and its indisputable superiority over bourgeois military science are convincingly borne out by the whole heroic history of our armed forces.

Marxism–Leninism is the sound ideological, theoretical and methodological base for Soviet military science. It ensures the correct understanding of the essence, character and peculiarities of wars and military development, of problems connected with training and with the conducting of hostilities, serves as a true compass in solving other current military problems and in determining the main trends in the further development of our military theory and practice. Comrade Brezhnev made a big contribution to Soviet military science.

The XXVIth Congress of the CPSU gave Soviet military science a new impetus. Guided by its decisions, our cadres are developing military science in accordance with the need to strengthen the country's defence, to improve the armed forces and in accordance with practical problems. They are concentrating much of their attention on deepening their knowledge of the most current and important phenomena in the military sphere and on broad scientific generalisation and the creative use of a large store of military experience.

Much has already been done in this respect, but still more is waiting to be done. The increasing complexity of the processes occurring both in social development as a whole and in military affairs requires Soviet science to penetrate ever more deeply into the character and peculiarities of modern warfare, to explain the mechanism of its laws and to interpret fully and constantly the regularities and tendencies in the development of armaments and methods for conducting hostilities. The timely elaboration

[7] V.I. Lenin, *Poln. sobr. soch.*, vol. 40, p. 183.

of scientifically-based ways for solving strategic, operational and tactical problems, the painstaking analysis and generalisation of advanced experience and a reduction in the time needed to put the fighting and operational training of troops into practice are all matters of growing importance.

It is impossible to understand what is occurring in military matters without a thorough study of past wars. It is likewise impossible without such a study to make a correct forecast of the future, to reveal the peculiarities of warfare using not only equipment that we already have but that which is planned for the future. It is no less important to study military matters abroad consistently and to analyse the changes that are taking place in the armies of the imperialist states.

Circumstances demand that we steadily strengthen and persistently develop and deepen the interrelationship between military science and the social, natural and technical sciences. Military science must be continuously enriched by the most effective research methods and achievements of the other sciences. One of the most important problems is the search for ways and means to increase the fighting might and preparedness of the armed forces as an indispensable condition for the reliable defence of our country.

Lenin's thesis that the point of view of real life and practice must be the prime and basic point of view of epistemology is widely known. Genuine science is based only on objective data reinforced by accurate experiment, by life itself and the strict verification of the scientific conclusions of practical work. Subjectivism, conceit and complacency are alien to it.

The purposeful application of scientific and technological advances also vitally affects Soviet military skill. An increase in the expansive range and dynamism of combats and operations makes it essential to work out and master new methods of conducting military action to correspond with the present-day level of armament development. The solution of this problem acquires no less significance than the creation and production of new weapons and *matériel*, the equipping of the forces and the competent handling of these armaments by personnel.

The military art will only live up to its purpose then if it reflects the fighting possibilities of the forces. In turn, their training must correspond to the requirements of the military art, its principles and conclusions. Success will ensure unity of theory and practice. In the final analysis the development and training of the armed forces are determined by this.

The development of the military art is a continual and complex process taking in all its fields—strategy, campaign tactics and tactics in general. The scope for strategy is increasing and the tasks connected with it are becoming more complex. Combat weapons have become more powerful and the rôle of strategic guidance in the training and direction of the armed forces greater. The framework of campaign tactics has also expanded. New principles for conducting combat action connected with improvements in *matériel* are being given prime consideration. Important qualitative changes are also taking place in tactics. New types of weapon help to secure reliable damaging fire, continuity of attack, the suddenness and swiftness of strikes, a constant combination of fire and manoeuvre and the excellent soundness and activity of defence.

All the component parts of the military art are to be found in dialectical unity. Their interrelated development is an indispensable condition for successfully solving the varied and complex problems contained in the structuring and training of the armed forces.

In our armed forces the development of military science and military skill is not only the affair of the governing personnel of the armed forces and of military scientists. In practically all the links of the army and navy organism officers are showing increasing interest in theoretical military learning and scientific research methods; they are leading the creative search for the most effective forms and methods of handling modern weapons, their optimal use and the best ways of conducting military action. The higher level of the theoretical-military and technical-professional training of officers and all personnel is helping to raise even further the useful results of this work. Combined organically with constant improvements in the technical equipping of the armed forces, it serves to increase steadily their military preparedness and to strengthen the country's defence capability.

3. Close Co-operation of the Fraternal Armies

The armed forces of the USSR, together with the armies of the other states of the socialist confraternity, are fulfilling their great historic mission of defending the gains of socialism and the cause of peace and social progress. In daily drill and service and the joint solution of tasks involving the security of the fraternal peoples and countries, the sociopolitical characteristic of consistent internationalism inherent in our armed forces from the first days of their existence stands out clearly and saliently. The fact that it is organically fused with ardent Soviet patriotism gives it especial force. Wherever a Soviet fighting man might happen to serve outside his country, wherever he might carry out his military duty—whether with some troops temporarily stationed in the territory of a fraternal state, or in a ship plying the expanses of the Pacific Ocean and paying friendly visits to foreign ports—he remembers everywhere and always that he is a representative of the Land of Soviets and personifies the honour and dignity of a Soviet citizen. The Warsaw Treaty Organisation has been the incarnation of proletarian, socialist internationalism in action for more than a quarter of a century. Lenin's ideas on the objective necessity for the close economic, political and military alliance of the socialist countries and on the obligatory consolidation of their economic, sociopolitical and strictly military possibilities for the reliable collective defence of the revolutionary gains of the workers have found embodiment and further development in it.

In its aims, tasks and character the Warsaw Treaty Organisation radically differs from the imperialist blocs which are destined for aggressive wars, the struggle against socialism and national liberation movements, against peace and social progress. The Warsaw Treaty Organisation is purely defensive, created for the protection of socialist gains from the aggressive encroachments of imperialism.

There is inherent in the military blocs of imperialist states, above all in NATO, an inequality between participants, the dominion of the strong over the weak, the urge of some states to secure their own selfish interests at the expense of others. In the Warsaw Treaty the principle of sovereignty is fundamental for those states joining it. This is clearly expressed both in the structure of the Warsaw Treaty Organisation and in the composition, terms of reference and order of activities of its chief political organ—the Political Consultative Committee.

As a voluntary, political-military alliance of free and equal states, the Warsaw Treaty reliably guarantees their sovereignty and security. That is the reason why all the fraternal parties and peoples look upon the reinforcement and development of these principles as a vital necessity, as their international duty. By carrying out this duty steadily and consistently, the socialist states take into account that imperialism is constantly increasing the power of its war machine. They cannot turn a blind eye to the fundamental changes which have occurred in the character of modern warfare and also to the fact that the imperialist aggressors are gambling on surprise attack.

The Warsaw Pact countries, in opposing the aggressive preparations of imperialism are maintaining the fighting might of the united armed forces, a high state of vigilance and constant readiness to repel an attack. This might draws support from the economic and spiritual potential of the socialist confraternity and serves as an insuperable barrier to the aggressive plans of imperialism which pose a threat to the entire world.

The goals of the political and military co-operation of the fraternal countries within the framework of the Warsaw Pact are noble. "We have created this community," said Comrade Brezhnev, "first of all to counter the threat of imperialism and the aggressive military blocs created by it, and in order to defend with our combined strength the cause of socialism and peace."[8] The XXVIth Congress of the CPSU marked their appreciation of the activities of the Warsaw Treaty Organisation when they emphasised that the political military defensive alliance of the socialist countries truly serves peace and has at its disposal all the essentials for the reliable defence of the socialist gains of the peoples.

The Warsaw Treaty Organisation is based on the common properties of the economic and sociopolitical régime, ideology and ethics and the fundamental interests and goals of the fraternal socialist states. The fraternal communist and workers' parties make up the core of their indestructible alliance, its living soul, figuratively speaking and its organising, guiding and directing force. They head the creative activity of the peoples who are building the new society, are tirelessly engaged in reinforcing the defensive might of the socialist countries and developing co-operation and military co-ordination between the fraternal armies.

The Committee of the Defence Ministers is doing much to ensure the co-ordinated development of the Allied Armed Forces. The Allied Command, the Staff HQ, and the Technical Committee of the Allied Armed Forces are playing an important part in this development. They are putting into practice the decisions that were reached at the Political Consultative Committee, are directing the activity of the Allied Armed Forces, working out and implementing specific measures for increasing battle training and preparedness and for strengthening the friendship and improving the co-ordination of the allied armies. The activities of these organs increases the effectiveness of the joint efforts made by the socialist states to ensure their collective security.

The co-operation of the armed forces of the Warsaw Treaty member states is developing in various directions. Co-ordination of plans for

[8] L.I. Brezhnev, *Leninskim kursom: rechi i stat'i*, vol. 4, p. 68.

developing the armed forces, and above all the conducting of a unified military and technological policy and the implementation of agreed measures for improving military preparedness, is one such development.

The allied armies generously share everything that is new between them, participate actively in working out the unification and standardisation of equipment. The manufacture of weapons and *matériel* is organised accordingly, making it possible to concentrate on the essentials and to economise on significant material and financial resources. An ever greater rôle is played by the international socialist division of labour, specialisation and co-operation in the defence industry and the co-ordination of scientific research and experimental design work in the military sphere.

Joint measures on military, political and operational training and the mutual exchange of experience in the instruction and education of fighting men cover another important area. The fraternal armies conduct joint operational strategic and tactical exercises. Problems connected with the training of commanding officers, staff and personnel are worked out in them, and improvements made in forms and methods of administration, the military co-ordination of army and navy forces, and the provision of *matériel* and equipment. Comradely relationships and friendships are strengthened and the traditions of fighting brotherhood added to. Joint exercises demonstrate the unity and cohesion of the allied armies and the high standard of ground, air and sea training for personnel. They serve as a real school for the patriotic and international education of the fighting men.

Joint courses, conferences and other similar arrangements also play an important rôle in helping the Allied Armed Forces acquire top experience in preparing the forces and instructing and educating personnel. Co-ordinated military and scientific work is carried out systematically, intensive research work is conducted on current problems and more effective forms and methods for using resources are investigated.

Primary consideration in the development of military science and skill is given to working out unified views on the character and methods of the combat activities of the allied forces. The contribution to military science from all the armies of the states—members of the Warsaw Treaty—grows with each passing year. The conclusions reached in Soviet military science, the very rich experience gained by the Soviet armed forces in combat and operational training and the training and education of personnel are all put to creative use in the fraternal armies.

Reciprocal aid in training the cadres of highly-qualified officers also serves to strengthen the military co-operation of the fraternal armies.

Widespread use of the highly-developed basic training of the Soviet armed forces and of the significant experience gained by them in the training and education of officers have helped to bring about a successful solution to this problem. There is much value to be had from training the military cadres in the other allied armies as well. All this is of assistance in steadily improving the officer training system in the armies of the Warsaw Treaty participant countries, in extending their co-operation and raising the fighting might of the Allied Armed Forces.

Co-operation among the political organs of the allied armies is constantly developing. They share their experience of party-political work and the patriotic and international education of personnel. Their activities are based on the directives of the communist and workers' parties of the countries of the socialist community which take into consideration both common international tasks and the national characteristics and traditions of each army. Cultural and sporting links between the fraternal armed forces are being strengthened.

Active and continuous work is going on in all these and other areas of co-operation. Such work brings the fighting men of the fraternal armies together that much closer, motivates them to give all their energies to martial labour which is intended to secure peaceful conditions for building the new society and reliable security for all the allied countries and the socialist community.

A steady devotion to the ideals of proletarian, socialist internationalism augments the moral political potential of the Warsaw Treaty Allied Armed Forces and increases the efficiency of this defensive organisation not only as a reliable guarantor of the gains of socialism but as an instrument of peace and international security.

The Soviet Union and the other Warsaw Treaty states are disinterestedly helping the liberated countries that have started out on the path to progressive development by defending their territorial integrity, independence and sovereignty. Imperialist propaganda is attempting to distort the extremely equitable character of this aid. However, despite its malicious fabrications, millions and millions of people in different corners of the world are seeing with ever greater clarity that the aid of the socialist countries has a progressive direction, is serving the goals of freedom and security for the peoples and is answering the real interests of all mankind.

Thus ever wider circles of the international community come to realise why the Afghan workers feel such gratitude for Soviet support. This support comes from real friends. It is dictated by loyalty to treaty obligations and is in response to the request of the government and friendly people of Afghanistan, serves as an expression of the sincere feelings of the Soviet people and the selfless fulfilment of the elevated, noble duty of internationalists.

The Soviet fighting men who, as part of a limited contingent of our forces, have the honour of rendering international assistance to the Afghan people are adding to the remarkable traditions of patriotism and internationalism in the Soviet armed forces by their daily deeds. These traditions are our wealth, our imperishable weapon. They are passed on from generation to generation and are of service in defending the workers' revolutionary gains. Today, as the intrigues of the imperialist and other reactionary forces make it essential for us to keep our powder dry and to work tirelessly on strengthening our joint defence, this weapon, as before, is in the right hands.

The attempts of the aggressive circles of imperialism and its accomplices to cause damage to the positions of true socialism and to the national liberation movement are doomed to failure. The Soviet Union and the socialist confraternity have, generally speaking, everything at their disposal to curb any aggressor. They are giving their unflagging attention to consolidating the Warsaw Treaty Organisation and to developing and extending the close co-operation between the fraternal socialist armies.

In their wholehearted devotion to the people, the Party and the communist cause the Soviet armed forces, in unison with the fraternal armies, are reliably defending the revolutionary gains of the working people and the security of peoples and peace on earth.

4

The Consummation of Military Skill

1. Towards New Heights in Military Preparedness

Our armed forces possess powerful fighting potential. To quote Comrade Brezhnev, it is a strong blend of high technology, military skill and uncrushable moral fibre. The capacity of the army and navy to realise this potential both quickly and fully against any possible aggression is reflected in their high military preparedness which is determined first and foremost by the excellent quality of training received by land, sea and air personnel, by their mastery of weapons and *matériel*, and the high degree of morale and political competence, discipline and organisation of the three services and their direction. In the final analysis, military preparedness, as Comrade Brezhnev emphasised, "is the consummation of the military skill of the forces in peacetime and the key to victory in wartime".[1]

The Party and its Central Committee in working out the main directions for improving the military preparedness of the armed forces as tasks of primary importance, are proceeding from the assumption that military preparedness in today's conditions must not only be maintained at a high level, but also continuously raised so that no unexpected occurrence might take us unawares. This need is brought about for many interrelated reasons.

In the first place there is an increase in imperialist aggression and an intensification of military preparations. The USA and its NATO partners in continually increasing their arsenal of aggression are intending it chiefly for

[1] L.I. Brezhnev, *Leninskim kursom*. vol. 2, p. 49.

the Soviet Union and the other countries of the socialist community. Hence the need for continuous improvement in the military preparedness of our armed forces. Wherever our troops may be stationed, their most important job is to find urgently the most effective methods and means for repelling aggression under conditions in which the enemy would be using all the possible means of war at his disposal.

This concerns, without exclusion, all aspects of the armed forces, all sorts of troops including special forces—those in communications, the railways, road transport, etc.—which have long ceased to be "auxiliary". But firstly the troops stationed on the foremost frontiers of our country and of the socialist confraternity who are on military duty must be in a state of high military preparedness.

The need for continuous improvement in the military preparedness of the armed forces is also dictated by the character and peculiarities of a possible war, and first of all by the increasing importance of the time factor. In the past, weeks and sometimes months were needed to get our forces and facilities ready to attack an aggressor. Under today's conditions this period of time can be counted in just hours or even minutes. The probable enemy possesses means of attack and groupments of forces that are capable of beginning military action at any time. Naturally this cannot but be reflected in the amount of time needed to carry out measures on military preparedness.

The necessity for further raising the military preparedness of the armed forces is largely predetermined by the increasing possibility of surprise attack. In the concepts of conducting war accepted by the armies of the imperialist states, stress is laid on the sudden "pre-emptive" strike. This, they calculate, will ensure the grasping of strategic initiative and superiority during the further conduct of war. And so our forces must be constantly prepared to repel aggression with maximum efficiency.

The duty of the Warsaw Treaty allies to defend jointly the gains of socialism demands a steady increase in the military preparedness of the Soviet armed forces. They must be constantly ready, shoulder to shoulder with the fraternal armies, to guarantee the security of the countries of the socialist confraternity and to protect both their national and common interests. This is achieved by carrying out agreed measures for improving the military preparedness of the armed forces of all the Warsaw Treaty countries.

Military preparedness is an excessively large-scale and complex affair involving much planning. It embodies the great efforts and material expenditure of the Soviet people towards equipping the armed forces with up-to-date weapons, *matériel,* and all the means and resources needed to keep them in peacetime and to guarantee their combat activity in time of war.

Military preparedness has a completely determined, specific content for each level in the structure of the armed forces, for every military collective and every fighting man, and the responsibilities involved in maintaining and steadily strengthening it are strictly regulated by laws and by other fundamental documents. The Soviet Constitution states that the duty of the armed forces to the people is to defend the socialist fatherland with reliability, and to be in a state of constant military preparedness, thus guaranteeing an immediate rebuff to any aggressor. The need to maintain constant military preparedness is included in the military oath and the service regulations. When taking the oath, every Soviet fighting man gives the solemn pledge that he will always be prepared to go to the defence of his fatherland—the USSR—and defend it courageously, skilfully, worthily and honestly, without sparing his blood or his life in achieving a complete victory over the enemy. The regulations governing the internal service of the Soviet armed forces require this. There is special emphasis on the personal responsibility of the commander to the Communist Party and the Soviet government to keep his sub-unit, unit or ship in constant readiness to fight and mobilise. Specific demands for maintaining military preparedness are made of every serviceman by military regulations, manuals, directives and orders.

The officer cadres have a decisive rôle in maintaining the military preparedness of the forces at the necessary level. They organise and direct the training, educational process and work of personnel. The successful solution of problems faced by the sub-units, units, ships and formations, and in the end the degree of the armed forces' military preparedness, are directly dependent on their precise work, mature thinking, professional preparation and ability to teach and to fuse together and to draw after them the military masses.

The sections responsible for keeping the forces in constant high military preparedness are entrusted to ensigns and warrant officers—the officer's closest assistants. These are highly-qualified specialists, real masters of their craft, who can skilfully handle the most complex *matériel* and have a great deal of experience in training and educating personnel.

The sergeants and petty officers—the most numerous contingent of the command cadres—contribute greatly to maintaining high military preparedness. Since they are constantly in the midst of the fighting men they are their immediate superiors, instructing and educating their subordinates on a daily basis, having an active influence on the reinforcement of organisation and discipline in the sub-units and successfully carrying out tasks involved with military and political preparation.

The act of raising military preparedness to the highest possible level is inseparable from the elevated moral, political and military qualities of personnel. As military affairs become more and more complex, the amount of training tasks increases, the character of martial work qualitatively changes and moral, psychological and physical commitments grow. All this makes great demands on the Soviet fighting man, on his ability to carry out his duties and his tasks connected with the crew, the sub-unit, the unit and ship successfully in any, even the most fraught and complicated, military circumstances.

A continual improvement in the military preparedness of the armed forces directly depends on how well personnel can handle the weaponry and *matériel*. A high degree of military preparedness is unthinkable without the ability of every fighting man and of every military collective to take from any model of modern weapon everything that has been put into its design, to make the best use of its possibilities.

The better the technical equipment of the forces, the more confidently personnel handle the weaponry and *matériel* and the more effective the methods for their use in battle, the higher the military preparedness of the sub-unit, the unit, the ship and the formation. This is one of the most important natural laws in the training of the armed forces.

Basic emphasis is put on mastering the latest weaponry and *matériel* in the forces. And this is right. But it should be remembered that the models of preceding generations are still in existence at the same time. This situation arises, on the one hand, because of the high rate of scientific and technological progress in military matters, and on the other hand, because of the impossibility of re-equipping simultaneously all the forces with new armaments. Therefore when teaching the fighting men to handle new weapons, it is important at the same time not to underrate the facilities that were in use earlier and still are in different units and ships. Personnel are obliged to make skilful use of the military possibilities of all models of weaponry and *matériel*.

Their military training, the ability to fight with modern equipment and achieve victories over a strong, well-armed and well-trained enemy make up the basis of military preparedness. Learning the rules of successful combat to win victories has never been a simple or easy matter. Now when the firing and striking power of the army and navy has grown immeasurably, when the character of battle has radically changed, it has become still more difficult to achieve a high standard of land, air and naval training and great daily efforts on the part of all personnel are required.

While perfecting combat training and military skill, we must always be on the watch for the probable enemy's new weapons and *matériel* and new tactical methods so that we can counteract them with new, highly efficient means and combat methods.

In order to improve military preparedness it is very important to achieve close co-operation between the different types of armed forces and special forces. Motorised infantry, tank crews, missile specialists, the artillerymen, anti-aircraft gunners, airborne troops, airmen and sailors have everything they need for the successful solution of whatever military problems may come up. But they would become that much stronger if their actions were co-ordinated, if their joint might were released on the enemy. Not a single military problem can be solved without the clearly organised and continuously maintained co-ordination of the various forces and weapons in modern combat.

Now that hostilities are characterised by their wide range and dynamic quality and that the forces are equipped primarily with collective types of weapons it is especially important that estimates, crews and sub-units be well co-ordinated in order to maintain military preparedness at the necessary level. This is achieved by a sure knowledge and the precise fulfilment by every serviceman of his duties, by well-developed mutual aid and a high degree of interchangeability among the fighting men.

In the preparation of personnel, it has become increasingly important to be able to solve problems during strong radio-electronic opposition from the enemy. A large rôle in improving military preparedness is played by full and versatile operational, rear and other types of security.

There is no such thing as a trifling or insignificant matter in the securing of military preparedness, for any mistake, miscalculation or delay in combat conditions, as a rule, is paid for in blood. Whatever position a fighting man may hold, he should always be asking himself whether he is capable of carrying out an order or is prepared to do so immediately; whether he has done everything he can to ensure the success of his military tasks by the sub-unit, unit or ship. Complacency and inaction are equivalent to retrogression and cannot be tolerated. Only relentless work, only ceaseless progression from each level gained to the next yet higher one can secure the necessary military preparedness.

The aggressive intrigues of imperialist reactionaries who are in the process of disposing militarily prepared groupments of forces and nuclear missiles that can be activated in just a few minutes greatly heighten the need for vigilance on the part of our armed forces' personnel. There can be no military preparedness without vigilance. "To keep on yawning or to lose one's head," wrote Lenin, "means to lose everything."[2]

Constant close vigilance must be practised by every Soviet fighting man. The responsibility of defending the fatherland that has been entrusted to the armed forces by the Party and people obliges the fighting man to be vigilant at all times and in all places: when carrying out combat duty, sentry and home duty, when working on military training and other problems, in the unit, the ship and elsewhere.

The XXVIth Congress of the CPSU noted with appreciation the military preparedness of the Soviet armed forces. We military people can be justly proud of such appreciation. At the same time it obliges us to give our unflagging attention to military preparedness and to conduct matters in such a way as to guarantee in advance the peaceable work of the Soviet people, and peace and security for the peoples.

2. Man—the Deciding Force

One of the most important tenets in Marxist–Leninist teaching about war and the army—the tenet about dialectical unity and the co-ordination of man and military technology—finds cogent embodiment in a high degree of military preparedness. A strictly defined rôle belongs to man and technology in this unity. Moreover the principal approach of Marxism–Leninism to evaluation of this rôle consists in the belief that man with his professional, moral, psychological and physical qualities occupies a commanding position in relation to technology at any level of its development. Military technology was always and still remains only a tool in military activity. And it is only due to the labour of man that it, like any other technology, has risen from the dead,[3] to quote Marx's words.

The appearance of new types of weaponry and primarily of nuclear missiles, the equipping of a whole number of armies with them and the

[2] V.I. Lenin, *Poln. sobr. soch.*, vol. 39, p. 55.
[3] K. Marx, F. Engels, *Soch*, vol. 23, p. 194.

widespread automation of control functions have not lessened man's rôle or the importance of his professional, moral, psychological and physical qualities. "However technically well-armed the army might be," said Comrade Brezhnev, "it is the man who has mastered the technology to perfection who becomes the chief, decisive force in war. This is especially important now in the age of the nuclear missile when it is the people who possess the weapons and *matériel*, who are mentally and physically tough and endlessly devoted to their country, Party and people who will decide the fortune of a war."[4] This conclusion is the creative development of the Marxist–Leninist view on the correlation of man and *matériel* as applied to the specific historical conditions of the present day.

The decisive rôle of man in combat is conditioned first of all by the peculiarities of modern warfare, the material preparation for which is being forced by the aggressive imperialistic circles. If these circles succeed in unleashing it, it will inevitably assume a character of confrontation between two opposing social systems of unrivalled bitterness and lack of compromise and will be a most severe test of man's spiritual and physical strength. The intensity of military activity will increase manyfold and the mental and physical burdens that will have to be overcome by personnel will grow markedly. In such conditions it is only possible to carry out successfully the combat tasks faced by the sub-unit, unit or ship, shoulder to shoulder with those fighting men who feel a very deep, unfaltering, to use Lenin's words "conviction in the justice of war and consciousness of the need to sacrifice one's life for the good of one's brothers . . .".[5] It is this conviction, this consciousness that is also being developed in the Soviet fighting men by the entire life-style of our society, by our armed forces and the purposeful work of the commanders, political organs and Party and Komsomol organisations.

If modern warfare makes excessively high demands on the fighting men generally, these demands are immeasurably greater on the officer. For the officer and, above all, the commander, must, like every soldier, stoically overcome the difficulties and dangers of combat. But first of all, he has to unceasingly and firmly lead the troops in all, even the most complex circumstances, to keep up the morale of his subordinates, to serve as an example of courage and fearlessness, to carry them with him and to inspire them to accomplish their tasks successfully. Hence the special need for a whole set of qualities that go to make up the modern

[4] L.I. Brezhnev, *Leninskim kursom*. vol. 2, p. 51.
[5] V.I. Lenin, *Poln. sobr. soch.*, vol. 41, p. 121.

Soviet officer. It is difficult to overestimate their importance and perhaps impossible.

Man's decisive rôle in modern warfare is also conditioned by the fact that the weapons by themselves cannot guarantee success. We need people for this—people who have a moral, political and professional training to match and who are capable, as Lenin remarked, "of profiting from the latest advances in *matériel* by knowledge of the matter".

The history of warfare abounds in examples of how well-equipped forces but with insufficient experience of their weapons have suffered defeat. But the opposite is also known to be true when first-rate military skill and handling backed by strength of spirit have made up for the inadequate technical equipment of the forces and secured victory.

They do not wage war according to numbers but to skill. This precept of Suvorov has not lost any of its actuality to this day. The ability to extract from the most complex modern armament everything of which it is capable, to operate it competently and to use it in battle with maximum efficiency creates preconditions for the successful solution of any military task. This ability presupposes, together with individual expertise, the highest level of co-ordinated action between many people—skilful, precise activities that are wholly subordinated to the united will of the commander and aimed at the achievement of victory in battle.

The modern fighting man should not only have a perfect knowledge of all the most effective ways of using the weapons and *matériel* entrusted to him, but should have a clear understanding of the tasks of the sub-unit, the unit and the ship and should know exactly what his place and rôle in the accomplishment of these tasks is.

Educating the fighting men to be highly organised and responsible is one of the most important areas in the work of the commanders, political organs, Party and Komsomol organisations. The key to success is here, confirmed by the respect and exacting nature of the mutual relations between fighting men, in their understanding that community interests are superior to personal ones, in their striving to carry out irreproachably both immediate service duties and all the combat and training tasks within the military collective.

This is especially important now when improvements in weapons and *matériel* call for an ever deeper division of military labour and give rise to new technological specialities. The operation and use of modern armaments demand the sort of professional training that can ensure mastery of any type of weapon and *matériel* in the shortest possible time and make it possible when necessary to take the place of a wounded comrade.

For the weapons and *matériel* to be under the control of the fighting men and for them to extract from them everything of which they are capable, knowledge alone is not enough even though extensive and comprehensive. Solid experience in the use of the equipment in the most difficult conditions of modern combat is also necessary. And since these conditions do not fit in, and cannot fit in with any standards, the creative thinking and initiative of the fighting men acquire primary importance. Along with a sense of discipline, courage, daring, selflessness and other qualities which always were and still are integral attributes of military valour, a capacity to act energetically, at full strength and over prolonged periods, is also required. In a word, our fighting men of today must be able, Comrade Brezhnev emphasised, "to bring together the traditions of selfless courage practised by their fathers with a complete knowledge of the latest *matériel*".[6] This would enable them to carry out worthily the responsible and honourable mission imposed on them by the Party and people.

The conceptions of the bourgeois theoreticians differ sharply from Marxist–Leninist views on the relationship of man to *matériel*. They put man and *matériel* in opposition to each other, attempt to look at them in isolation from the specific sociopolitical environment and historical situation. Here some make the rôle of the weapons absolute, especially nuclear weapons, and put forward ways to automate them as if for a species of "higher beings" which would be capable of taking man's place. Such absolutisation of weapons and *matériel* serves, for all intents and purposes, to justify the increase in armaments and at the same time the training of men who carry out orders unthinkingly and the transformation of the soldiers in the imperialist armies into a peculiar sort of appendage to the modern weapon.

Other bourgeois military theoreticians advance concepts in which absolutisation of the weapon and *matériel* goes side by side with the forced acknowledgement that man is still the basic tool of war. Similar conceptions have even recently been reflected in the official documents of the imperialist armies. This is connected with the fact that attempts to oust man from the control of *matériel* and forces with the help of the computer has proved fruitless. However, recognition of man's most important rôle in war does not by any means signify that the imperialists have given up their intention to turn the personnel of their armies into a blind instrument of anti-democratic, aggressive and reactionary policy. Cruelty, contempt for man, his dignity, for his life itself and for any of the values of

[6] L.I. Brezhnev, *Na strazhe mira i sotsializma,* 2nd ed., Moscow, 1981, p. 235.

civilisation are propagated by any and all means among the servicemen. The ideological handling of the personnel of the US armed forces and their NATO partners is carried out in a spirit of militarism and aggression, of anti-Sovietism and anti-communism. And it bears its sinister fruits. The crimes of the American soldiery during the aggressive war in Vietnam, the atrocities of the British troops in Ulster and the massacres perpetrated by the Israeli murderers in the Middle East are evidence of this.

By graft and falsehood, by political infiltration and purges, by the strict preservation of the bourgeois caste system in the officer corps—by all these and other measures—monopolistic capital makes the army of the masses its obedient tool. Equipped with the latest armaments these armies are a serious force destined to defend the reactionary interests of the bourgeoisie. But because this force is in opposition to the people it is devoid of effective ideological, moral and political drive. In consequence of this, as the facts of history show, the armies of the exploiter states will not, in the final count, stand up to the grave moral and psychological stresses, will go to pieces in difficult situations and lose their capacity to fight. This has invariably happened in the past. It is all the more real in today's conditions.

There is not, nor can there be, in the armies of the exploiter states that phenomenon which constitutes the chief property of the socialist armies and is the life-giving source of their indestructible might. That is, the justice of the goals which the socialist armed forces are serving and their truly human destiny which answers the fundamental interests of the working masses. We are naturally also talking about the personnel of the socialist armies who are ideologically tough and limitlessly devoted to the people and the socialist fatherland. Only socialism gives rise to mass heroism and self-sacrifice. "The strength and virility of the Soviet armed forces", Comrade Brezhnev remarked, "are based on an acute awareness by all servicemen of their patriotic duty, their profound ideological conviction and boundless faith in the ideals of communism. This menacing weapon of our army has, from the first days of its existence, always helped it to conquer the enemy."[7]

While carrying out its daily leadership of the armed forces, the CPSU gives its unflagging attention to this powerful spiritual weapon and takes care of it continuously so that the ideological, political, moral, military and psychological training of the fighting men might always be on a level with the greatest demands of the time.

[7] L.I. Brezhnev, *Na strazhe mira i sotsializma,* p. 104.

3. Raising the Efficiency of Troop Control

The military preparedness of the armed forces is directly dependent on the standard of leadership, on the skill of commanders, staffs and all the administrative organs to organise and unite the personnel and to mobilise its energy and will to solve the problems before it. Efficient control means the unconditional achievement of the goals set and a more rational use of the military possibilities of the sub-units, units, ships and formations. To do this we need to find our bearings in events with certainty, to forecast how situations will develop, to work out well-grounded plans, to make expedient decisions and put them persistently into practice.

Even a superficial enumeration of the demands made on control shows what qualities a military leader needs to possess. These qualities, it goes without saying, do not come of themselves. They are acquired through persistent study and continuous independent work in the course of daily activities. The creative application of progressive methods and means of control, a penetrating interpretation of military experience and a complete knowledge of all the best that has accumulated from the most useful practice in training the forces and in instructing and educating personnel are of primary importance.

Improvements in the control of the armed forces are carried out in conformity with the general demands made by the CPSU on leadership in all areas of communist construction, in all Party, Soviet and economic cadres. "Rights—extensive rights—are granted to leaders that they might make full use of them," said Comrade Brezhnev at the XXVIth Congress of the CPSU. "But here every leader must always remember his great responsibility—his responsibility to the people whom he has been entrusted to lead, to the Party and the nation".[8]

The responsibility of the military leader for the skilful administration of the forces is unprecedentedly high in present conditions. This is due to the fundamental changes that have taken place in the ways and methods of conducting war. Even with adequate technical equipment and well-instructed personnel, the military possibilities of the sub-divisions, divisions, ships and formations will not be properly utilised and the execution of tasks will be under threat of disruption if the administration is not reliable.

It is the same when achieving the goals of an operation or combat; the rôle of administration is equally important when working on tasks of

[8] *Materials from the XXVIth Congress of the CPSU*, p. 50.

military and political training and military preparedness. The more purposeful and efficient it is and the more completely it answers present needs, the better will be the results of the tasks performed. The most important conditions for efficient control are a broad introduction to the scientific organisation of labour and to the foremost planning methods and an active use of modern computing technology.

But it would be mistaken to consider that fulfilment of these conditions would automatically guarantee success. One may make a correct decision, set up a good plan and put forward an excellent idea. But if they are not properly organised when put into practice, they will remain dead. Nothing happens by itself. The people who envisage a goal, who know how to achieve it and have the required knowledge, experience and resources to follow it up decide all. It is not by chance that our Party looks upon administration as the science of work with people. To master it means to have mastered the science of victory. And for this every officer needs to raise his level of Marxist–Leninist preparation with energy and persistence, to expand his operational and tactical field of vision and to improve his ability to act in difficult and tense situations.

Based, as it is, on the general scientific foundations and Leninist principles for the administration of socialist society, the theory and practice of administration of the forces have at the same time their own peculiarities. They are conditioned by the specific character of modern warfare, as is the task of protecting the socialist fatherland and military activity.

A profound knowledge of the laws of war, a full consideration of their influence and forms of manifestation under specific conditions are of use in determining correctly the major and most important trends in the development of military matters, in making a proper assessment of the situation and its possible changes and in making more expedient decisions. In other words, by drawing on a knowledge of the laws of war, by letting oneself be guided by the fundamental principles and methods for administering the forces, it is possible to foresee the development of events and at the same time to ensure, to a large degree, the successful accomplishment of necessary tasks.

Foresight is of great importance in all spheres of man's activity. Lenin valued it as an indispensable quality in correctly determining the basic trends of social development. Possessing the invaluable gift of foresight himself, Lenin revealed the sources and intrinsic interaction of the most complex events and processes occurring in society and predicted with scientific authenticity the possible paths of their further development. The entire history of mankind in the twentieth century is confirmation of the brilliant perspicacity of our great leader.

Foresight in the military sphere plays an enormous rôle. And this is understandable. The price of error and miscalculation is too great here—it is a question of security for our country, the soundness of its defence and the ability of the armed forces to deal any aggressor a crushing blow. Here errors in evaluating the possible development of events, in determining the priority of tasks and the relative importance of different work trends as well as mistakes in decisions taken are especially dangerous in today's conditions. This is primarily because the scale of the probable consequences of these miscalculations and errors has grown immeasurably. Putting them right has become much more difficult, and sometimes impossible.

Today the importance of foresight in strategic, operational and tactical leadership and in decision-making has become greater than ever. It is impossible, without it, to prepare the forces for successful action. That is why, obviously, it would not be an exaggeration to say that administration in today's conditions implies first and foremost an ability to see ahead. If the major developmental trends in the military sphere, the level achieved and the prospects for growth of the economy, the sociopolitical and spiritual development of Soviet society and the achievements of scientific and technological progress were not taken into account, the effective administration of the structuring and improvement of the armed forces would be impossible. No less important is a timely and objective evaluation of the strengths and possibilities of the probable enemy giving consideration to trends in changes. Success in solving the problems before the forces depends a great deal on the ability to see what the prospects are when training the sub-units, units, ships and formations and to ensure that they correspond not only to today's needs but to those of tomorrow also.

As an integral part of the scientific approach to the organisation of instruction and education of personnel and to the preparation and conducting of a modern operation or battle, foresight acquires a special significance in relation to the presence among the forces of powerful, high-speed, long-range means of fire, of their high technical preparedness and also in view of the necessity to make the best possible decisions, as a rule in extremely compressed periods of time and in tense, speedily and abruptly changing circumstances.

It is quite obvious that a decision will only be expedient if it is based on painstaking operational and tactical calculations, on a deep and full analysis of the situation, on an exact reckoning of the position, condition and possibilities of one's own forces and those of the enemy, of the developing alignment of forces, the radiation situation and the local, meteorological and other conditions. Generally speaking, decision-making is always a difficult creative process, always some kind of step into the unknown. Every decision in some measure or another is bound up with risk in so far as it is more often than not based on incomplete and at times contradictory data and is under active enemy influence. However, risk is by no means a random action made in the hope of a beneficial outcome to the battle or operation. On the contrary, it is the ability to discover the hidden factors in a situation and having worked out the enemy's way of thinking, to anticipate it and to foist one's will on him.

However complex the problem involving foresight may be it is possible to solve it successfully. In order to do this, military leaders of all ranks must persistently work on ways of fully analysing situations, and must bring to light what is important and what can determine the course and outcome of the battle or operation. It is also very important to work doggedly on the ability to reconstruct a general picture of events from separate, at times seemingly trivial details and to select corresponding methods of military action and forms of manoeuvre to anticipate the enemy's intentions, ensure the effective use of one's own strengths and resources and to make good use of all the available possibilities to achieve success.

Foresight enables one to organise administration better, to ensure that the projected battle or operational plan is put into practice and decisions implemented. But all this should be with highly reliable and stable means of communication and the proper efficiency of the administrative organs. Here at least three aspects may be borne in mind. Communications must be concealed, protected from enemy interference and stable irrespective of the difficulties in the radioelectronic situation. Otherwise it is impossible to have control in contemporary warfare. Firmness and flexibility in troop control is likewise important. Even the best decision may turn out to be impracticable if administration is not firm. At the same time flexibility and efficiency make it possible to introduce expedient changes at the right time in the original plan of action, to anticipate events and channel them advantageously for us and disadvantageously for the enemy. And finally, it is essential to organise in a rational way the activities of the command echelons and the skilful deployment of forces and weapons in relation to control points.

In modern conditions the commander and staff have, as a rule, considerably less time than in the past to organise combat. And the volume of information on the situation has grown immensely and continues to grow. One can say without exaggeration that there is a serious and acute problem here. There are two ways to solve it. The first is to improve the operational and tactical training of the commanders and staffs and the second is to automate control of the forces even further. Both these answers are of course organically interlinked. And success can only be guaranteed if they are implemented.

Continued improvements in the operational and tactical training of commanders and staffs are a decisive precondition to achieving a high standard of military preparedness for all the echelons of the command system. It goes without saying that all the measures in this sphere must be based on the growth of the general and military culture of the officer cadres and be reinforced by the solid practical experience of troop controls. It is a question of knowing how to work out solutions in short periods of time and to carry out preparations for battle, to clearly set out the tasks to be performed and to organise co-operation during the battle or operation.

Automation of troop control would serve these goals. It would significantly speed up the gathering and processing of information, and the preparation of data for decision-making; it would be of use in optimising planning and in bringing military tasks, orders, signals and commands to the forces in good time. As a result of the introduction and skilful use of automation, the commanders and staffs would gain additional time for creative work in the course of preparing and conducting military action. At the same time troop control would become more efficient.

In discovering the great opportunities for overcoming the contradictions between the growing demands on administration and the possibilities of fulfilling them, automation on its own, of course, would not guarantee efficient control of the forces. Its introduction should be combined with well-thought out organisation of the activities of the administrative organs. In their turn, these activities should be guaranteed in technical, mathematical, informational and all other respects. In particular the simulation of an operation or battle based on mathematical methods significantly extends the possibilities of foresight, makes it possible to consider more precisely and completely the numerous factors influencing the course and outcome of military action. Calculations for strategic operations, operational forecasts, military economy and technical and tactical matters draw from these methods. The best possible versions of plans for complex measures are worked out with their help, graphs can be drawn to find the most rational work for the various organs of administration and the precise co-ordination of strengths and resources and the reliable control of implementation are achieved.

But even with a high degree of automation the chief rôle in troop control will always belong to the commander, and the HQ, as before, will still be the basic command echelon organ. That is why it is so important to develop initiative as much as possible as well as the creative activity, independence and sense of responsibility of the military cadres and leadership and to inculcate progressive methods of planning and decision-making. Improvement of the style of troop control activity is closely connected with improvements in the structure of the command echelons in all areas—strategic, operational and tactical.

Our officers, political and engineering cadres are persistently enriching their theoretical arsenal and improving on their practical experience. They are in step with the times, possess excellent professional training and strong moral fibre and are capable of solving any, even the most complex, problems involved in efficient control of the forces.

5

Training and Education

1. Studying the Real Way

Improvements in weapons and *matériel*, forms and methods of combat and reinforcement of the rôle of the moral political factor in modern warfare make great demands on the quality of instruction and education of personnel. These demands are related to both those who organise the educational process and are in daily charge of it and those who are being taught, who are called upon to master the martial skills and to become stout and skilful defenders of the socialist fatherland.

Their joint activities and common purpose in steadily increasing the military preparedness of the armed forces provide a guarantee of excellence in training and education.

Training and education in the services is a two-in-one process. It is primarily concerned with the preparation of fighting men with awareness and excellent military, moral, political and psychological qualities and with the military co-ordination of sub-units, units and ships. The basic efforts of the officer cadres and of the entire personnel are concentrated in these areas.

Lenin's slogan "Study military matters the real way!" now serves Soviet fighting men as a guide to practical action. By following it they acquire a whole mass of ideological, political and professional military knowledge, learn how to handle weapons and *matériel*, and can work out how best to be prepared and act in any military conditions. The rational use of training time, the economising of means and resources, the continuous search for and familiarisation with such forms and methods of training as answer in large measure modern needs are the immediate concern of every fighting man and every military collective.

In the forces quite a number of measures are passed with the aim of increasing the effectiveness and quality of instruction and education. Such attention is fully justified. However, it is not always positive experience that is spread. Decisions and recommendations are not always put into practice. What sometimes happens is that people talk together, look at something and then go their own ways—the matter is then dropped. Obviously little benefit is to be derived from such measures. Anything of value should not only receive approval but be generalised and included with some urgency in the military and political training and education of personnel. This is all the more important in view of the fact that educational plans and programmes are becoming fuller from year to year and the problems before the fighting men more complex.

Consistent practice of the Leninist principle of communist integrity, of Party teaching and education, the creative application of the conclusions and recommendations of military science and skill and of military teaching and psychology play a primary rôle in increasing the effectiveness and quality of the educational process. It is important to have a good knowledge of the real state of affairs in the sub-unit, unit or ship, to have correct, timely and full information about the lives and activities of personnel. Lenin highly valued the ability "to give oneself the most accurate account of the state of affairs without closing one's eyes to the truth".[1]

Clever planning occupies an important place in the work of increasing the effectiveness and quality of instruction and education. It goes without saying that in any part of the army or navy organism and at any level of structure of the armed forces the plan must be real and its implementation assured on all sides. This does not just mean in the material and technological aspect but in the organisational and ideological sense as well. Strict observation of the requirements of planned discipline are of especial importance. Here it is important to make precise arrangements for checking the work and controlling its performance. To command without following up performance due to lack of interest or ability, wrote Lenin, "is absolutely ruinous in military matters".[2]

A skilful overall approach to solving problems of military instruction serves to increase the effectiveness and quality of instruction and education. As applied to the armed forces, an overall approach presupposes the

[1] V.I. Lenin, *Poln. sobr. soch.*, vol. 36, p. 366.
[2] V.I. Lenin, *Poln. sobr. soch.*, vol. 51, p. 50.

indissoluble unity between the instruction of personnel and their political, military and moral education. It makes it possible to get the greatest return from the use of teaching time and material resources, to form excellent fighting, moral, political and psychological qualities in the fighting men, to arm them with essential knowledge and experience within short periods of time and to achieve military co-ordination among sub-units, units and ships.

It is not possible to talk seriously about increasing the effectiveness and quality of training without constantly improving the forms and methods of instruction and education. They must not lag behind the changes occurring in the technical equipment of the armed forces and the methods and ways of conducting military action. Quite a number of questions crop up before us here and in particular that of the growing complexity of organisational problems in co-ordinating the many different strengths and resources in the battle or operation. Quite naturally it has become extremely difficult to express today's educational process in a single, permanently set methodical formula. And there is hardly a need for this. No single method or form of instruction and education, taken separately, can guarantee the high-quality training of servicemen, and even more so of the sub-unit, unit or ship. Something else is important here. We need to apply widely and creatively both the traditional forms and methods of instruction and education that have been tested by life and the new forms which have arisen from daily practice in the services. We can only achieve the increased effectiveness and quality of the educational process in these conditions.

In this regard, the great importance of combat experience, especially that gained in the Great Patriotic War, in the instruction and education of fighting men should be mentioned. This is our invaluable wealth. And the ability to use it to solve problems is a vital indication of maturity in an officer. Experience of contemporary local wars also merits attentive study.

Along with experience of warfare the experience gained from daily combat and political training and especially of extensive manoeuvres and exercises should be widely used. But this experience can only be really useful if all the combat and political training, and even more so, the manoeuvres and exercises, are carried out in conditions as close as possible to the real thing. In other words, the forces need to be taught what is essential in warfare. This today is an indisputable condition of good military preparedness and it must be strictly implemented. A great amount of work is being done in this direction and it is giving positive results. The "West-81" exercises that took place in September 1981 gave particular proof of this. Matters of military co-ordination and co-operation were given a work-out in them when joint military actions with formations and units were carried out. The fighting men who participated in the exercises, discharged their duties honourably. They showed courage, the ability to act with energy and initiative and to use their weapons in battle with skill. The exercises revealed highly-developed political maturity, the remarkable, tough qualities of the personnel and their readiness to defend selflessly our socialist fatherland and our friends and allies.

The "West-81" exercises were an examination in martial skill in which the forces gave account of their successes in military and political training to the Party, government and Soviet people. The General Secretary of the Central Committee of the CPSU, President of the Praesidium of the USSR Supreme Soviet, President of the USSR Defence Council, Marshal of the Soviet Union, Comrade Brezhnev, highly appreciated the actions of the forces during the exercises. "Excellent training, the precise co-ordination of types of forces, the skilful mastery of formidable modern technology," he emphasised, "all this was demonstrated during the exercises."[3]

Generally speaking, a careful, attentive attitude to the experience that has been amassed is an important condition for certain progress. Naturally this experience has to be applied creatively, with consideration given to the specific conditions in which the sub-unit, unit or ship may be solving the tasks ahead of them, the specific features of the kind of armed forces and type of forces involved and the peculiarities of the weapons and *matériel*.

Improvements in the forms and methods of instruction and education of fighting men demand creativity and initiative, purposefulness and persistence. It is important to gather something new from the grains, to check this out from all angles and develop it further. It is obvious that resounding phrases are not necessary here but laborious daily work instead which would exclude both any irrelevance that would impede new thinking and any attempt to introduce an undertaking without a serious explanation of its real use simply noting indiscriminately what was applied before.

With such a variety of forms and methods for instructing and educating personnel the goals set can only be reached when educational matters are worked on with full exertion. The state of and prospects for development of military matters, the conditions of the theatre of operations, the fighting efficiency of one's own troops and those of the potential enemy and his

[3] *Pravda*, 16 September, 1981.

and his weak and strong aspects must be reflected in the content and character of the educational process.

These are some of the general demands made on the educational process. Certain attitudes connected with specific practical work in instruction and education of personnel result from them.

The following are indispensable conditions for the effectiveness of the training process, and again the "West-81" exercises showed this clearly; these are: its clear-cut organisation, instructiveness, the creating of circumstances which demand the full exertion of spiritual and physical powers, maximum performance, and initiative and creative thinking on the part of the fighting men. It is no secret that indulgence and over-simplification seriously harm the quality of instruction and education. They are especially intolerable because they impede the correct preparation of fighting men for modern combat and can create a false impression about it. And this is fraught with negative consequences in an actual combat situation.

In the final analysis, it is the readiness and ability of the fighting man to carry out competently and skilfully the duties imposed on him in any combat conditions that is the main, decisive indicator of the efficacy and quality of the educational process. What this indicator will be depends greatly on the ideological and professional level and the methodical mastery of the command, political and engineering cadres.

To teach and educate subordinates one needs to know and be able to do a lot of things, to be erudite and have a good general culture. One needs to know not only what, but how to teach and to possess a whole arsenal of teaching and educational methods and to apply them creatively. Today one of the basic criteria for the methodical skill of the teacher is the ability to bring the greatest possible amount of knowledge to the students and to give them solid experience in very compressed periods of time. And this is natural. For the demands on the preparation of a fighting man are steadily growing and the duration of terms of service have not changed. As experience shows, a successful solution to this problem is achieved thanks to a continuous appraisal of the actual level of personnel training, of the character of the problems before the sub-unit, unit and ship, the priority and conditions of their fulfilment and the concentration of basic efforts on the chief trends and areas in the work of instructing and educating fighting men.

Naturally a concentration of basic effort on the chief trends does not in any way mean that other matters can remain outside the officer's field of vision. The skilful leader and educator of subordinates will divide his attention properly and will never lose sight of the so-called "trifles". These same "trifles", if ignored, can grow by degrees into serious omissions.

Work with people constitutes the very heart of teaching and education. Attainment of educational goals depends directly on the ability of officers to organise the activities of their subordinates, to give them a purposeful character and to draw support from Party and Komsomol organisations and the military collective. Mutual understanding between superiors and subordinates, the co-ordination of their actions and a general desire to solve the tasks before them are of great significance here.

Unfortunately, some commanders and superiors are inclined to think that to be successful it is necessary to maintain a certain distance between themselves and their subordinates and to be exacting towards them—these considerations are based exclusively on the system of superiority. There can be no doubt that the military man must unconditionally observe the system of superiority. But it must not be forgotten that an exacting attitude is only really efficacious when it is combined with respect for subordinates and comes from trust in them. "Trust", said Comrade Brezhnev, "inspires people, gives them added strength and confidence."[4]

The confidence of the fighting man in himself, in his strength and capabilities, in his comrades, shoulder to shoulder with whom he is carrying out his military service, and of course in the commanders and superiors, under whose leadership his entire activity passes, is a great help in solving combat-training and educational problems. The richest practice of our armed forces shows that success accompanies those officers who not only teach their subordinates but learn from them themselves, who at all times develop a feeling in the fighting men of their own worth, encourage initiative and creativity and listen to their opinions. Where the commanders, political workers and all the officers know the mood of their personnel, its spiritual and other needs and its strong and weak aspects and can skilfully combine the individual approach with support from the collective, there is invariably a high standard of military and political preparation; socialist obligations are discharged and firm order and strong military discipline maintained. This dependence has a natural character about it which is daily and hourly confirmed by reality.

In the hands of the organisers and leaders of the educational process this is a truly powerful means of increasing its efficacy and quality. It is conditioned by the sociopolitical nature of our armed forces. This is

[4] L.I. Brezhnev, *Leninskim kursom,* vol. 2, p. 206.

socialist competition. Comrade Brezhnev called it one of the clearest manifestations of the new attitude to work. Being essentially an embodiment of the awareness, initiative and creativity of the Soviet people, socialist competition penetrates all the links of the educational process in the armed forces. Organised in conformity with the Leninist principles of publicity, the comparability of results, the full use of top experience, it mobilises fighting men to find good solutions to combat and political training problems, motivates them to equal the top performers[5] and class specialists, to work with maximum efficiency without resting on their laurels but rather going unfailingly forwards and reaching for what is important. Socialist competition in the forces today takes in practically all personnel and is directed at putting into practice the resolutions of the XXVIth Congress of the CPSU.

In accordance with the resolution of the Central Committee of the CPSU, the USSR Council of Ministers, the All-Union Central Trade Union Council and the Central Committee of the All-Union Leninist Young Communist League "on all-Union Socialist competition for the successful fulfilment and overfulfilment of tasks for the eleventh five-year plan" in military districts, groupments of forces, fleets, formations, units, ships, military educational establishments, military undertakings, military institutions and organisations—everywhere in the armed forces—measures are being planned and carried out guaranteeing further elevation of the rôle of socialist competition by promoting quality solutions to the problems of military and political training and the raising of military preparedness. Commanders, political organs, Party and Komsomol organisations are striving with all sorts of ideological educational work to add to the splendid traditions of socialist competition, to create in each collective the right conditions for real creative search, competition, comradely help, a well-developed sense of responsibility and efficiency. They obtain in return the effective support of the servicemen, workers and employees in the services and a broad spread of initiative directed at further increasing work efficiency and quality and achieving good end results in teaching and educating personnel.

It is quite evident that a higher degree of efficiency and quality in education cannot be attained without full use of the educational technical base and its continued development. There are in the forces educational centres, training grounds, shooting ranges, classes, laboratories and training complexes. They ensure that such pursuits and training as combat

[5] *Otlichniki*—those who get top marks, e.g. "excellent" (*Translator*).

shooting, practical missile launchings and bomb dropping are carried out to a high standard. However in order for the educational technical base to match up to modern demands, it must be constantly developed. This relates, in the first place, to means of communication, the introduction of electronic apparata, various optical, mechanical and other devices and appliances and simulation equipment.

The efforts of designers and inventors in industry are directed at making new complex aviation, missile, tank and other training devices and simulators for firing which record the results of target-hitting and other training equipment. The efficiency experts and inventors in the armed forces make a considerable contribution in this regard. There are many opportunities in the forces for the independent manufacture and widespread distribution of many types of training devices, of simulators and other equipment which are of help in broadening the educational process. It is important to make fuller use of these opportunities.

The continual growth of the general educational and cultural level of personnel create an opening for the widespread use of technical means of programmed instruction. This creates good preconditions for reducing the time spent on training the specialist fighting man, economising on energy, means and resources and in the end raising the effectiveness and quality of the whole training and educational process.

Development of the educational technical base makes it all the more expensive. And this is natural. For, as you understand, it is equipped with complex instruments, devices and equipment. Thanks to the unceasing concern of the Party and the Soviet people, the fighting men have all they need for productive military training and service and for a full-blooded spiritual life. It would be over-zealous to refer to everything that the Soviet people give the armed forces—this requirement results from the general directive of the XXVIth Party Congress on the need to take good care of national property. The Soviet fighting men see this as a guiding principle in daily life and activity.

There is a direct link between the effectiveness of the training and education of personnel and the level of military discipline. Good organisation and firm order give the forces the ability to act quickly, clearly and co-ordinatedly in any situation, to come forward with a basic, timely, strict and exact implementation of educational plans and programmes and to achieve the best possible results from every pursuit, every study period. At the same time, even the odd occurrence showing lack of organisation can lead to serious slip-ups in military and political training. It can have a most negative influence on the quality of study and can do considerable harm to the cause of education. Consequently, the stronger the discipline in the sub-unit, unit or ship, the greater the efficiency and quality of the educational process. There is, of course, a feedback circuit here for the better the training and education of the fighting men, the greater the effect they have on strengthening discipline. Our officer cadres should always take this dialectical dependency into consideration in their daily activities. A further increase in the effectiveness and quality of the educational process in the armed forces is guaranteed by the friendly, co-ordinated work of the commanders, political organs, Party and Komsomol organisations and by the selfless work of all personnel.

2. The High Calling of the Officer

The difficult and responsible work of the Soviet officer is surrounded in our country by general honour and esteem—this work is done in the name of the Soviet people's freedom and happiness and their radiant future, in the name of peace and life on earth. The new man of socialist mentality is a man of the people to his very bones, the people's loyal and devoted son; the Soviet officer is nurtured and educated by the Party in a spirit of unwavering devotion to the cause of communism and to the principles of proletarian, socialist internationalism. The officer's calling is a guarantee of the reliable defence of the socialist fatherland. He gives all his strength, knowledge and talent to this high calling.

The Soviet officer cadre has a remarkable history. Its origins go back to that stormy time when the newly-emerged Soviet Republic was forced to fight for its freedom in the cruel struggle against internal and external counter-revoution. Even then, on a day in the difficult year of 1919, Lenin, turning to a future commander of the Red Army, predicted that the Red officers who came from the people, "will have authority among the soldiers and will know how to strengthen socialism in our army. Such an army will be invincible."[6]

The correctness of Lenin's prediction has been convincingly confirmed in reality. Through numerous fights and engagements Soviet officers have borne their high calling with honour. In the heroic annals of the Soviet armed forces the names of the first Soviet military leaders, commanders and political workers are inscribed in gold letters—S.M. Budyennyi, K.E.

[6] V.I. Lenin, *Poln. sobr. soch.*, vol. 37, p. 200.

Voroshilov, S.M. Kirov, V.V. Kuibyshev, M.N. Tukhachevskii, M.V. Frunze and many other heroes who have laid the foundation for the new, socialist fighting traditions—the traditions of wholehearted, selfless service to the Soviet fatherland.

These marvellous traditions were continued and added to during the Great Patriotic War. The feats of N. Gastello and A. Mares'ev, A. Pokryshkin and I. Kozhedub, I. Panfilov and L. Dovator and thousands of other officers and generals at the front have become clear symbols of the unbending strength of the spirit, the will to victory and military skill. A weighty contribution to the increase in our fighting traditions and to the treasure-house of Soviet military skill has been made by a new galaxy of commanders and military leaders who have been educated by the Party—G.K. Zhukov, A.M. Vasilevskii, I.Kh. Bagramyan, N.F. Batutin, L.A. Govorov, A.G. Golovko, A.I. Eremenko, I.S. Konev, N.G. Kuznetsov, R.Ya. Malinovskii, K.A. Meretskov, K.S. Moskalenko, F.S. Oktyabr'skii, I.E. Petrov, K.K. Rokossovskii, F.I. Tolbykhin, I.D. Chernyakhovskii, V.I. Chuikov and many others. Hundreds of thousands of generals, admirals and officers have been awarded orders and medals of the USSR and more than six thousand have received the award of Hero of the Soviet Union for their great military skill, courage, stoicism and heroism.

And now, in peacetime, Soviet officers are worthily carrying on this heroism and glory and selfless loyalty to their patriotic and international duty. The Soviet people, the peoples of the fraternal socialist countries hold sacred in their memories the young pilots of one of the airforce units of a group of Soviet forces in Germany, officers B. Kapustin and Yu. Yanov who sacrificed their own lives to steer their falling plane away from some highly-populated residential areas. Lieutenant A. Kiselev showed self-control and composure in a moment of mortal danger. In saving the lives of his subordinates, he lost both his hands. Now a young officer he again finds himself in the service of the armed forces and is studying in the military academy. Captain N. Kuznetsov of the technical service did not retreat before death, saving as he did a wheatfield from incineration. First Lieutenant V. Goncharenko perished while carrying people out of a fire. Officers also set examples of heroism, courage and daring in their daily service and training. Many are awarded military decorations and the cream of the cream receive the award of Hero of the Soviet Union.

The continuity of the generations, which is characteristic of our socialist system and Soviet way of life, gives a special unity to the officer corps of the armed forces and augments its spiritual potential. Each new generation of commanders, political workers, engineers and technicians takes what is best from its predecessors, draws on their experience and, thanks to this, achieves further improvements in training and an increase in the military preparedness of the forces.

It is a great honour to be an officer of the Soviet armed forces. It is also a huge responsibility. The people entrust their sons to the officer. During the time of their actual service in the forces young people pass through a good school of life under the direct leadership of commanders and political workers, become mentally and physically tough and acquire political, military and technical knowledge and essential experience. The coming into being of the fighting man and his maturing depend to a decisive extent on the knowledge, professional and teaching skill and personal example of the officer.

A basic part of the complex and varied professional activity of the officer is to ensure a high degree of military preparedness among the forces. This demands constant self-discipline on his part, an ability to subordinate his own needs and interests to the interests of military duty. It would not be an exaggeration to say that an officer's life is one of daily, unseen, humdrum heroism; it is the highest civic spirit, patriotism and internationalism in action.

The great importance and exceptional responsibility of the job given the officer by the Party and people, make great demands on his moral, political, professional and business-like qualities. The Soviet officer is a man who is selflessly dedicated to the Communist Party and his people, who possesses a profound knowledge of Marxism–Leninism, broad political vision and good general culture. He is a man with all-round professional training, elevated moral fighting qualities, who knows to perfection the military possibilities of his weapons and how to use them. This military leader who skilfully draws for his work on the collective and who uses up-to-date methods for training and educating subordinates is capable of organising their work and inspiring them to follow him on an exploit.

It is the communist ideology that constitutes the foundation of the Soviet officer's lofty moral, political and business-like qualities. His firmness and consistency in carrying out Party policies, his politically conscious attitude to his military duty and his exacting attitude to himself and others is based on it. It determines the spiritual stamp of the officer, his feelings and will and penetrates all his deeds and actions. An inner self-discipline, faithfulness to his word, an ability to keep his composure and self-control in any situation and a readiness and ability to carry out an order precisely and in good time distinguish the Soviet officer. It is not by chance that we associate our ideas of a strong will, irreproachable sense of organisation and discipline, initiative and a creative approach to matters with the image of the officer. All these qualities of the officer have a beneficial influence on his subordinates and the military collective and enable him to achieve good results in his educational work.

The heroic history of our armed forces and their daily reality show how great and truly invaluable the personal example of the officer is when carrying out his military duty for the successful solution of military tasks and the tasks of training and educating personnel and for strengthening military discipline. The officer does not nor cannot have real authority without this, and this also means real success in his work.

Generally speaking no post of itself brings authority and respect. The authority of the post is not equivalent to the authority of the man who occupies it. And the person who thinks that authority will be guaranteed automatically with his appointment to some post or other is deeply in error. It is not for nothing that the people say: it is not the position that adorns the man, but the man the position. That is why it is important for him to think constantly about how he can justify trust and live up to the position he is holding by his labour, his organisation, ability and concrete achievements in raising the military preparedness of a sub-unit, unit or ship. That is the only way to gain real authority.

But it is still not everything to have gained authority. He has to reinforce it constantly with deeds but not just in his official capacity. There are quite a number of facets to the authority of the leader which acquire special significance in the armed forces. The subordinates follow the example of the officers: during wartime—in battle, and in peacetime—in drill, service, communal organisation and in way of life. It is therefore particularly important for the moral climate of the military collective and for the success of all officer activities that the officer be efficient, morally pure, modest, that he should have a caring, comradely relationship with his subordinates and an ability to win them over. Continuous lively contacts with his subordinates help the officer to find the true path to their hearts. And the man who can possess the heart of a soldier possesses the secret of victory.

There is probably nothing more harmful to an officer's authority than a discrepancy between his words and deeds or a retreat from ethical norms. Rudeness, conceit and self-assurance are also inimical to authority as are faint-heartedness, indecisiveness and attempts to be playful with subordinates. Real respect does not include any kind of familiarity. It is in its own way no less insulting than arrogance. Equable, comradely relations with subordinates do not exclude the rigorous execution of all the demands of the seniority system. They presuppose at the same time deep mutual understanding. However erudite, talented and efficient an officer may be he will never be able to head a collective either formally or in actuality and lead his subordinates effectively without their support and the ability to direct their will, energy and knowledge to the achievement of common success. "A communist leader", wrote Lenin, "should only demonstrate his right to leadership when he finds many, and still more and more, helpers . . . when he knows how to help them work, to promote them and to reveal and take their experience into consideration".[7]

This ability presupposes, besides everything else, the leader's competence. Soviet officers are highly educated people with a broad professional training. The foundations of their education are laid in military educational establishments and these foundations are reliable and solid. But it is the school of practical activity, the school of life itself that turns out to be the chief school for every person. And in order to be in step with its demands an officer needs to replenish tirelessly and from day to day his store of political, scientific, military and specialised knowledge, to perfect his experience and to plan ahead. Unfortunately we still meet with individual officers who have ceased to grow ideologically and professionally and are content with the volume of knowledge they have acquired at some time. And they justify this by being busy and not finding opportunities for systematic independent study.

What can be said in this regard? As a rule, in fact, the officer does not have very much time to do independent study. This means that he has to make rational use of his time, to learn how to pick out what is most important and vital in a job, since the effectiveness of the educational process and the quality of problem-solving in the sub-unit, unit or ship primarily depend on this. No less important is the ability to plan his work concisely, to organise it and to allocate his time and energy properly. The scientific organisation of labour starts with this.

The correct organisation of the officer's activities must combine a well-thought-out individual plan for the working day with the most rational allocation of time to the varied assortment of duties he must perform on a daily basis within the sub-unit, unit, ship, staff or institution. This is all

[7] V.I. Lenin, *Poln. sobr. soch.*, vol. 42, p. 325.

the more essential since increasingly complex problems have to be solved in very limited periods of time and, as a result, not only the higher standard of his own training but, in no less a measure, the effectiveness and quality of training and education of personnel are dependent on the officer's rational use of time and energy. Unimportant surveillance, the substitution of junior with senior people and the cases of unnecessary duplication and double insurance that are met with at times have nothing in common with proper organisation.

It is, of course, not simple to learn how to organise one's work and the work of one's subordinates properly. A very prominent rôle in the solution of this problem belongs to the military educational establishments. They must lay the basis for the officer's good personal sense of organisation, dispose him to take an enterprising and creative approach to matters and to round out and renew his knowledge persistently. The senior commanders, political organs, Party and Komsomol organisations are ceaselessly called on to take on the job of strengthening and developing such qualities during the entire term of the officer's service. But the chief condition contributing to the success of the officer's activity and his continuous growth is the unflagging work he puts in on himself, the purposeful and unceasing improvements he makes in his own knowledge and experience.

For those officers who are inquisitive, energetic and have initiative, wide scope for self-improvement and for mastering the heights of military and specialised knowledge is opened up by combat duty, exercises, flying, naval cruises, training and studies, in the process of which many questions to do with the familiarisation and use of weapons and *matériel* and the organisation of educational work are studied and solved in new ways. It can be said with full assurance that it is only the officer who persistently studies over the whole term of his service, works on improving his knowledge and experience and applies them creatively to his everyday activity who finds himself on top of the needs of the time and is successful in instructing and educating his subordinates and in directing the sub-unit, unit or ship.

The results of the officer's work are directly dependent on his clever use of the enormous influence of the Party and Komsomol organisations in the interests of solving the problems of combat and political training and strengthening discipline. The commanders of sub-units, units and ships who are members of the CPSU and form an absolute majority of our officer cadres, draw support in their work from Party organisations and channel their activity into the successful execution of combat tasks, combat and political training plans and the strengthening of military discipline. The commanders who are not members of the CPSU, must also work in the closest association with Party organisations, draw support from them and make extensive use of the experience of the communists and the strength of Party activists in solving all these problems.

The commanders in directing the activities of the Party organisation and drawing support from them, set a personal example by their active participation in the life and affairs of the Party organisation, help develop criticism and self-criticism, listen carefully to the advice and suggestions of the communists, uphold their initiatives, make use of their experience and bear the fact constantly in mind that the Party should in fact be the cementing and mobilising force in the military collective.

The ability to draw support from the Party organisation and to direct its activity does not come to the officer at once. He needs experience and political maturity for this. That is why the concern over the making of officers, especially young ones is so important, as is the concrete, businesslike daily work of the commanders, political organs and Party organisations in inculcating in them a well-developed, personal sense of responsibility towards the irreproachable performance of duties. Naturally, every officer has his own particular duties and to a certain extent his own individual style of working. It can not be otherwise for there is no single recipe for how to act "on every occasion". But there are general requirements to be met by everyone. Of first importance are mastery of the Leninist workstyle, a responsible attitude to one's duties, a high-principled outlook, unity of word and deed, an exacting nature and at the same time a sensitivity towards people and their material and spiritual needs.

Soviet officers are persistently learning up-to-date methods of leadership and raising the efficiency and quality of their work. They are mobilising the fighting men to put the resolutions of the XXVIth Congress of the CPSU into practice, heading the martial work of their personal staff directed at putting programmes and military and political training plans into action, and taking care of socialist obligations and tasks set the armed forces by the Party and people.

As people with a highly-developed sense of duty, of remarkable ideological, political, professional and moral qualities, Soviet officers like all the personal staff of the armed forces, are closely rallied around the Communist Party and its Central Committee. They give their energy and knowledge to steadily increasing the military might and preparedness of the armed forces and to strengthening the country's defence capability.

3. With the Full Force of Party Influence

Comrade Brezhnev called party political work the powerful tool of our army. "The power of this weapon", he emphasised, "has been tested in the fire of battle. Our enemies are scared of this weapon."[8]

Imbued as it is with Lenin's ideas on the defence of the socialist fatherland, party political work with its characteristic means and methods motivates fighting men to carry out their patriotic and international duties irreproachably and to solve the tasks before the armed forces. It deeply influences the consciousness and feelings of the personal staff, unites the military collectives and makes it possible to raise the level of leadership in the forces. It occupies the most important place in the educational rôle of the armed forces.

The importance of party political work in the services is steadily growing. This is due to the increasing complexity of the problems associated with the training and military preparedness of the armed forces and with the sociopolitical and technical peculiarities of modern warfare which makes greater claims than ever before on the moral, political and psychological toughness of the personal staff.

The forms and methods of party political work are improved from year to year. The work is conducted taking into account the special features of the different categories of personal staff and in organic association with the specific tasks of the forces as well as with the conditions in which the fighting men live and work. Increased efficiency in party political work serves to concentrate the co-ordinated efforts of the commanders, political organs, Party and Komsomol organisations on the major directives to come out of the XXVIth Party Congress and on the resolutions of the Central Committee of the CPSU "on the further improvement of ideological and political education work" of 26 April 1979 and other Party documents.

One of the major tasks of party political work in the services has been and still is to form a scientific outlook in the fighting men, to instil in them wholehearted devotion to the cause of the Party and to communist ideals as well as socialist patriotism and internationalism. Finding support in the unshakeable basis of Marxist–Leninist teaching, this work is called upon with all its forms and methods to arm the personal staff with a profound and clear understanding of the laws of and prospects for social development. The reasoned propaganda of the enormous advantages and achievements of

[8] L.I. Brezhnev, *Leninskim kursom,* vol. 2, p. 51.

socialism and the socialist way of life constitutes yet another most important trend in party political work. It must along with this unmask, in an energetic and convinced fashion, the reactionary, anti-democratic essence of imperialism and its home and foreign policies, any anti-Soviet tendency in its military preparations and instil a high degree of political vigilance in the personal staff and a clear understanding of their responsibility for the reliable defence of the gains of socialism and the preservation of peace on earth.

The military part of party political work consists in educating the fighting men in the revolutionary, military and working traditions of the Communist Party, the Soviet people and our armed forces. It is impossible to imagine the present-day life of our services without the constant lively contacts of the personal staff with the veterans of the Party and armed forces, with the Heroes of the Soviet Union and the Heroes of Socialist Labour and those who took part in the Civil and Great Patriotic Wars. The word of a veteran—who is the living personification of the legendary glory of the armed forces—has a great influence on the mind and heart of a young fighting man. The activities of the veterans and of those who continue to serve in the forces, those who are working in the different sectors of communist construction and those who are now having a well-earned rest, require the constant attention and support of the commanders, the political organs and Party and Komsomol organisations of the armed forces.

The evenings of military glory that are organised in the sub-units, units and on ships play an educational rôle as do study sessions and excursions by military units and formations to museums and places of historical fights and battles. As a rule, all these measures which are notable for the highly emotional effect they produce, turn into real lessons in courage, stoicism and loyalty to patriotic and international duty. A big, very important and necessary job is done by those commanders and political workers who strive to make sure that every fighting man might know the military path of his regiment, ship or formation, might feel proud that he has been given the honour of serving under a battle flag so covered with heroic glory and be aware of his personal responsibility for worthily continuing and augmenting the martial valour of the older generations.

Our armed forces are rightly called the school of patriotism and socialist internationalism. Every military collective thinks of itself as a friendly, united military family in which representatives of different nations and nationalities of the Soviet Union serve together. The spiritual links that bind them are solid and indissoluble. The military friendship of the Soviet fighting men with those of the armies of the fraternal socialist states is imbued with a spirit of internationalism.

The real patriots and internationalists, the fighting men of the USSR armed forces, as all the Soviet people, demonstrate their class solidarity with the world communist and working-class movement and with those who fight for social and national liberation. They understand that the martial work of the fighting men of the Country of the Soviets is in the name of peace and social progress.

All areas of party political work are indissolubly linked and complement and enrich each other. And they all need to be directed at achieving end results which will best help to bring about steady improvements in the training of the forces, the strengthening of discipline and organisational ability in the fighting men and the increased military preparedness of the armed forces.

It is quite obvious that party political work cannot produce results if it is carried out in isolation from the life and activities of the forces. Its effectiveness depends directly on the topicality of content, on the matching of forms and methods of work with the educational and general cultural level of the fighting men. Our time is one in which the scale and complexity of the problems being solved by the Soviet people are growing enormously. At the same time it is a period of extremely acute ideological confrontation between socialism and capitalism. And it is very important in party political work not to go round these so-called difficult questions that arise but to meet them in good time. For if we do not face up to these types of questions then as Comrade Brezhnev emphasised at the XXVIth Congress of the CPSU, "the enemies of our country will try to profit by them to slander socialism".[9]

Of course it is not easy to discuss sensitive subjects. It is necessary in such cases to be competent and to be able to reveal the class essence of phenomena and facts and to unmask lies, misinformation and forged documents with conviction. The ideological front is not called the front of the struggle for people's minds and hearts just by chance. And every commander, political worker and officer must master the art of taking the offensive and winning on this front. It is the honourable and responsible job of all who carry the ideas of the Party to the masses and explain its policies and organise and conduct party political work to instil class consciousness in the personal staff and an irreconcilability to alien views and

[9] *Materials from the XXVIth Congress of the CPSU*, p. 75.

ways and to reinforce on a world-wide basis the active and vital position of the warrior citizen, patriot and internationalist.

The efficacy of party political work also depends to a large extent on what consideration is given to the new tendencies in it and the peculiarities of development in military affairs and changes in the qualitative state of the forces. It is necessary to always bear in mind the moral, psychological and physical ordeals that the personal staff may have to undergo in modern warfare and to conduct party political work in such a way that it would actively help to increase the reserves of military, ideological and moral stoicism of the personal staff. The fighting man's practical actions and particular acts in difficult circumstances are the main indicator to his ability to overcome all difficulties and privations in the name of performing a military task. One should base oneself on this when planning and organising party political work and evaluating its status and results.

The richest experience of our armed forces testifies to the fact that party political work is all the more productive, the stronger its links with the military training of the forces. Today an increasingly significant place in party political work is taken up by matters relating to the handling of modern weapons and *matériel* by personal staff, to raising the quality of military training, increasing the useful output of every hour of training and every pursuit and economising on means and resources.

The immutable rule of party political work is continuity. Breaks in it, for whatever reason, are inadmissible, and its activity must be directly proportional to the complexity of the situation and problems to be solved. Moreover the active nature of party political work is not gauged by the number of measures being planned and carried out. The decisive criteria here is the power exercised by the constant and effective Party influence on all aspects of the lives and activities of the fighting men.

The art of achieving such influence is revealed with impressive depth and conviction in Comrade Brezhnev's book *Little Land*. When relating experiences of party political work in wartime conditions, Comrade Brezhnev remarked:

> "Resounding speeches were not necessary here, in fact there were no halls for speeches, but frank, manly and, I would say, sincere conversation instead. I took part in the majority of Party meetings conducted in military formations and units and often mixed with the fighting men. I usually managed to find a common language with the soldiers and sailors although I did not employ any particular

methods for this. Whether the conversation was light-hearted or serious I tried to behave simply and equably. And I always spoke the truth however bitter. I noticed that there were among the officers those who tried to project themselves as straightforward fellows. The fighting men, of course, immediately felt the falsity of this deliberate familiarity and could not then expect them to be frank.

"Most of our political department heads, political instructors, Komsomol organisers and agitators knew how to find the right tone, enjoyed authority among the soldiers and it was important that people knew who would call upon them in difficult times to stand their ground, stand alongside them, remain with them or go ahead of them with weapons in their hands. Probably our chief weapon was the impassioned Party word reinforced by the deed—personal example in battle. That is the reason why the political workers have become the moving spirit of the armed forces."[10]

It can be said without exaggeration that this excerpt from *Little Land* gives a clear idea of the standard of really effective party political work and of the qualities that should be possessed by the people who take it to the masses.

The natural closeness of the commanders, political workers and all the officers to the soldiers and sailors which originates in the socialistic nature of our armed forces enables them to have a good knowledge of the spiritual and material needs, interests, positive aspects and shortcomings of subordinates. Here an experienced officer will know how important it is not just to confine himself to military service. A thoughtful study of the lives of his subordinates before they enter the army is especially important for successfully developing the necessary moral, political and fighting qualities of personnel. The firm links established by the commanders, political workers and Party and Komsomol organisations with the parents of the fighting men, the educational establishments, the collectives of enterprises, state and collective farms and the institutes from which young people go straight into the army and navy have a significant educational impact on this plane. These links which form one of the elements of indissoluble unity in our army and navy make it possible to ensure continuity in the young person's education, to draw on the best in himself to help in forming the personality of a protector of the socialist fatherland.

The officer's deep and comprehensive knowledge of his subordinates, his ability, to use Lenin's words, to win their boundless trust, at the same time

[10] L.I. Brezhnev, *Na strazhe mira i sotsializma*, p. 560.

maintaining a comradely relationship with them and attentively satisfying their needs, are necessary conditions for effective Party influence on personnel. It is only by knowing people, drawing on living relationships with them and on their trust and support, that one can achieve the high moral tone of personnel and inspire them to selfless martial labour and the irreproachable fulfilment of military duty.

It is obvious that without a knowledge of the individual peculiarities of people, their inclinations, enthusiasms and place and rôle in the collective one cannot plan one's party political work properly. Since this work is closely bound up with the problems which personnel are trying to resolve, it introduces a political principle into the organisation and content of military training, into the development of socialist competition and the struggle to steadily raise military preparedness.

The Party organisations are the political core, the cementing strength of the military collectives in our armed forces. The results of party political work depend to a great extent on their activity and fighting spirit. The ideological and organisational activity of the communists, their living word and the example they set in fulfilling their military obligations stand out as the major factors of Party influence on the masses of the fighting men.

From the very beginnings of our armed forces the communists have been in the front ranks of our fighting men. They are always to be found in the most difficult places where success is being forged. To be out in front is the one and only privilege of the man with the party ticket in his breast pocket. This was pointed out even as far back as the VIIIth Congress of the Russian Communist Party (of Bolsheviks) when it was emphasised that being a member of a communist cell did not give a soldier any special rights but only imposed an obligation on him to be a highly selfless and courageous fighter. The communists of the armed forces are steadfastly true to this elevated duty. Both now and in the past they set an example by the irreproachable way in which they carry out Party and military duties, and by their tireless efforts to perfect ideological toughness and professional skill; they stand against complacency and lack of drive and are in favour of bringing unused reserves and potentialities into operation and steadily increasing the vigilance and military preparedness of the forces.

The Komsomol organisations provide reliable and loyal help to the Party organisations of the armed forces. They contribute a good deal to moulding the young fighting men who have left their factory benches, collective farm fields, colleges and schools to enter the army and navy. And the activity and fighting quality of the Komsomol organisations in the sub-units, units and ships do much to make the young fighting men feel that they are supported by the collective from the very beginning of their service and to develop in them a firm belief in success and a desire to continue and add to the achievements of their predecessors.

Quite naturally the novices meet with many difficulties at first. They cannot get accustomed straight away to the strict life-style, to the intensive pace of military work and the demanding nature of military service. The overwhelming majority of soldiers quickly overcome these difficulties. But it sometimes happens that things do not go smoothly for a recruit. It is important in that case to give timely encouragement to the person and if necessary to set him right, not to let him stumble and to help him occupy a worthy place in the glorious service of the armed defenders of the socialist fatherland.

Party political work in the Soviet army and navy actively helps to solve all the problems faced by the services. The persistent struggle of the fighting men for good, stable results in training and service, for the satisfactory fulfilment of socialist obligations and the further improvement of military preparedness is evidence of the effectiveness of this work and the steady strengthening of Party influence on all aspects of the life and activities of personnel.

Conclusion

The Soviet people under the leadership of their experienced fighting vanguard—Lenin's Communist Party—have been tirelessly and consistently putting the historic plans outlined at the XXVIth Congress of the CPSU into practice. They have been augmenting the economic and defensive might of the country with their urgent work in all the different areas of communist construction. From day to day the international positions of the Soviet Union have been growing stronger and the beneficial influences of its constantly peaceable and firm foreign policy has been spreading.

The armed forces of the USSR are reliably standing guard over the peaceful labour of the Soviet people, the great gains of socialism and peace on earth. They make up an organic part of the developed socialist society and are inextricably bound with the labouring masses. They embody the best features of our people. The Soviet fighting men are ideologically strong, can handle masterfully the formidable weaponry and *matériel* of today and carry out their duty with honour.

The defence capability of the USSR and military preparedness of our armed forces are on a par with today's requirements. This results from the consistent and steadfast policies conducted by the CPSU and the Soviet state in which there is an indissoluble merging of creative and defensive tasks with a peaceable outlook and at the same time a perpetual readiness to repel any aggression resolutely. Carrying on these Leninist policies, the XXVIth Congress of the CPSU has adopted a comprehensive programme for further communist construction and has demonstrated the adamant resolution of the Communist Party and Soviet people to defend peace.

The threat to peace, and this threat is serious, originates from the aggressive powers of imperialism and reaction. They are attempting in any way they can to hamper the objective course of mankind's progressive development. Under the false pretext of "the Soviet military threat", the warlike circles of the USA and NATO are speeding up militarist preparations in order to destroy the military strategic balance that has taken shape in the world, to attain the unattainable—military superiority over the USSR and the Warsaw Pact. They are stirring up tensions in different areas of the globe, are conducting unbridled psychological warfare against real socialism, the national liberation movement and all the forces of peace and progress.

All this demands a high degree of political vigilance and an active and resolute struggle to preserve *détente* and the consolidation of universal peace by the Soviet people, the peoples of the fraternal countries and all progressive mankind.

The Soviet Union is at the forefront of this struggle. By demonstrating firm political will and boldness and a realistic, far-sighted approach to present international problems, it is persistently striving to avert the threat of war and to strengthen security for the peoples. The new, important peaceable initiatives put forward at the XXVIth Congress of the CPSU have received wide international acknowledgement and support like the Peace Programme for the Eighties.

Our allies and friends—the countries of the socialist confraternity—are proceeding shoulder to shoulder with the Soviet Union to construct the new society and to work for its defence and the cause of peace. This combination of efforts helps resolve both national and international problems and objectively answers the fundamental interests of all mankind.

The indestructible unity and fruitful co-operation of the countries of the socialist confraternity are a great gain for the fraternal parties and peoples, our common property. It will steadily increase and grow stronger. The Warsaw Treaty Organisation is of service in defending with reliability the great gains of socialism and peace.

The Soviet armed forces carry out their patriotic and international duty in the united fighting structure of the fraternal armies. They have at their disposal all the essentials with which to resolve the tasks imposed on them. The Soviet fighting men repay the care of the Party and people and the love and trust of the workers with their selfless martial labour. In battling together with all the people to put the plans outlined at the XXVIth Congress of the CPSU into action, they are persistently increasing the effectiveness and quality of military and political training and tirelessly reinforcing the vigilance and military preparedness of the armed forces.

The Soviet people can be assured that their offspring—the armed forces—is always on guard, always on the alert, and always ready to repel aggression wherever it may come from. The Soviet fighting men who are educated by the Party and closely united around it, are carrying out their duty with honour and serving their country and the cause of communism with devotion and selflessness.

Index

Index